I Love You, Sign Here

Contracts for Couples

Roy & Sarah Pierson

Regan Arts.

NEW YORK

Regan Arts.
New York, NY

Copyright © 2017 by Roy Pierson and Sarah Pierson

First Regan Arts paperback edition, November 2017.

Library of Congress Control Number: 2017937179

ISBN 978-1-68245-090-1

Cover design by Richard Ljoenes
Interior design by Nancy Singer

Printed in the United States of America

10 9 8 7 6 5 4 3 2 1

PART 6:

Health and Wellness

PART 7:

Food and Dining

PART 8:

Entertainment and Outings

PART 9:

Family and In-Laws

PART 12:

Pets, Friends, Kids, and Exes

Introduction

Hey! Look at you two gorgeous weirdos reading a book together. How adorable. And smart, because you're about to get 'er done for once—all with the help of this zany little book!

Aren't things the best in Coupleland? Modern life is so cozy, what with all the streaming shows, myriad essential oil diffuser options, soggy sandwiches delivered right to your bunker by UberEats, etc. While the outside world is a big, scary shit show that gets freakier by the day. But all things are calm in your little love cocoon. Wait. No? What's the problem? Hit a flat note in your relationship? Are you having the same fights day in, day out about the same mind-numbing BS?

Our precious Interwebz have trained us all to be impatient, annoying, and . . . um, wait . . . what . . . I'm just . . . ? Oh, yeah, easily distracted. How are we supposed to maintain loving, real-life relationships while taking advantage of this gilded age of accessible "information" (i.e. porn, fake news, bogus Wikipedia entries, deep plunges into your coworker's fiancée's Instagram, ruses for the complete disintegration of your privacy and dignity by delusional dorks like Zuckerberg and Bezos, etc.)? Between spending more than half your life "working" and gluing your face to your phone, you only have so much actual time to spend together. Do you really want to spend it bickering? Of course not. Plainly no. *And how!*

Well, fear no more, lovers. Get ready to put it all in writing and resolve every utterly predictable conflict in your coupledom! Whenever you get "all jammed up," you need only to whip out this handy book, customize the appropriate contract, sign on the dotted line, and slap that son of a bitch on the fridge.

If you guys are really going to crush it, here's a tip: Back away from the screens (we know it's hard, but grow up), focus for more than six seconds (nearly impossible, we know), talk face-to-face and actually acknowledge your partner. After all, isn't that what life's about? I mean, kind of? *In a way?* And the next time one of you wants to buy a 90-inch 3-D LED television or a tricked-out white-noise machine, you or your partner can (affectionately) exclaim, "Check the contract, dumbass! We're broke, you moron! Love you!"

DISCLAIMER: The contracts presented in this book are not intended for use in an actual court of law. The authors do not assume any legal liability for your divorce/breakup/imprisonment. Please don't sue us if your relationship falls apart. In fact, proper execution of the contracts contained herein should bring you closer together and strengthen the foundation of your relationship by fostering communication and accountability therein. Or maybe we're just saying that to cover our asses. No, it's true, and we will take full credit for your new #RelationshipGoals status.

PART 1:
Money

Don't blame your significant other for their vintage troll doll next-day-delivery online ordering addiction. They clearly have no self-control and a serious—albeit endearing—brain malfunction (which is one of the reasons you love them, right?). Try out the following contracts and see if you two lovebirds can agree to save some cash. You might even celebrate your commitment to save by having sex! That *should* be a freebie in a romantic relationship. (Before engaging in any sexual acts, you are advised to execute contract #3.1 on page 27.)

☐ 1.1 THE FINANCIAL LITERACY CONTRACT (HERE IS HOW MONEY WORKS)

☐ 1.2 THE BANNING OF EXPENSIVE AND IDIOTIC PURCHASES CONTRACT

☐ 1.3 THE SPENDING FREEZE CONTRACT

☐ 1.4 THE GOIN' DUTCH CONTRACT

1.1 The Financial Literacy Contract (Here Is How Money Works)

Agree to be smart with finances and learn how to understand basic concepts like APR, budgeting, how a mortgage works, investment strategies, and payment due dates. And also agree not to day-trade marijuana stocks, cotton, or oil futures.

_____ (Partner 1) and _____ (Partner 2), hereinafter referred to as "the Couple," hereby declare they will not be huge morons when it comes to financial literacy and agree to enter into the "This Is Money, This Is Important" contract on _____, the ____ day of the month of _____, in fiscal year _____. This contract requires each party to acquire and *retain* a minimum threshold of financial literacy and prohibits any massive financial blunders, such as missing due dates and watching passively as your credit card interest rate explodes like a rocket launch funded by some a-hole billionaire megalomaniac, signing up for an unneeded credit card (including Kohl's, Men's Wearhouse, Cheesecake Factory, etc.), and _____ _____ (enter as many as you need here, which will be many if you're dummies like us).

Both parties agree not to run up massive amounts of credit card debt in order to "rack up awards points," which allow said dummy to use his/her "rewards" to purchase uncomfortable, circulation-blocking, hideous argyle socks at a slight discount online from the Gap, which is in dire financial straits itself, most likely caused by not using debt appropriately (and having sucky items). Ironic, isn't it? Metafinancial idiocy, you might call it . . . if you were an asshole.

This contract will expire on _____, after which the Couple may choose to quiz each other on how much of an idiot they still are / are not when it comes to money matters and then most likely renew the contract indefinitely, as the stakes should go up the longer you stay together (most people earn more money as they get older, but who knows, the way things are going, you may fall into the wealth gap!). Never mind the fact that the word "gap" is appearing a lot in this contract; there is nothing subliminal going on. We do not work (directly) for the Gap. Face it, you are getting very old, and one day you might want to retire. Right? Or just keep working until you die because you love working so much that it isn't really "work"? STFU and just sign.

I HAVE READ THIS AGREEMENT; I HAVE TAKEN TIME TO CONSIDER ITS IMPLICATIONS; WE DON'T WANT TO DIE IN A SOUP KITCHEN, ESPECIALLY NOT TOGETHER; I FULLY UNDERSTAND ITS CONTENTS (I THINK), I AGREE TO ITS TERMS, AND I VOLUNTARILY SUBMIT TO ITS EXECUTION.

_____
Partner 1

_____
Partner 2 ("2" indicates inferior status, based on gross income)

1.2 The Banning of Expensive and Idiotic Purchases Contract

Return the $400 white-noise machine, $500 dumbbell set you've never picked up (too weak), and $1,400 deluxe, as-seen-on-TV incline treadmill you've used only once!

_____ (Partner 1) and _____ (Partner 2), hereinafter referred to as "the Couple," hereby declare they will restrict moronic purchases, hereinafter referred to as "the Infomercial Ban," on _____, the ____ day of the month of _____, in the year of our Lord ____. The Ban prohibits any and all large, extraordinarily foolhardy purchases, especially ones made without the consent of the other partner, that exceed a fat price tag of _____.

The Ban will expire on _____, after which the Couple may consult with one another on a single must-have-or-can-no-longer-live purchase, such as matching Foosball tables, most likely fake and worthless Ancestry DNA tests, artisan fur capes, high-end bean bag chairs (they exist and are insanely comfortable; rich people who can afford such luxuries would be well advised to purchase several), or the registration of binary stars (sounds kind of cool, actually). If both parties are in agreement, the purchase may be made, after which another Ban shall be immediately reinstated (because you have no self-control and limited intelligence), expiring on _____.

Moreover the Couple agrees to forgo the dippiest of all joint couple expenses: a huge, scary wedding. Unless there is a psycho parent or tenuous health situation in play, the couple agrees to save their money for something practical, like Google Glass (Defunct yet? Haven't heard, and don't care enough to take the four seconds to check) or an electronic drum kit.

I HAVE READ THIS AGREEMENT, I HAVE TAKEN TIME TO CONSIDER ITS IMPLICATIONS, I KNOW WE WILL NEVER USE A WAFFLE IRON OR ANY EXERCISE EQUIPMENT IN OUR HOME MORE THAN ONCE (OR TWICE, IF WE GET REALLY DRUNK), I FULLY UNDERSTAND ITS CONTENTS, I AGREE TO ITS TERMS, AND I VOLUNTARILY SUBMIT TO ITS EXECUTION.

_____

Partner 1

_____

Partner 2

1.3 The Spending Freeze Contract

Let's just take a step back and ease up on our cash burn rate for a month or so. Cash burn . . . that's a thing, right?

_____ (Partner 1) and _____ (Partner 2), hereinafter referred to as "the Couple," hereby declare they will commence a spending freeze, hereinafter referred to as "the Freeze," on _____, the ____ day of the month of _____, in the year of our Lord _____. The Freeze prohibits any and all purchases outside basic necessities (defined as groceries, work expenses, life-sustaining and/or flatulence-preventing medications, _____, _____, _____), with a dispensation for _____ (and pizza, of course) from _____(specify authorized restaurant) one day per week (you still gotta live a little, right?).

The Freeze will expire on _____, thus totaling ____ days/ weeks/months (months? are you freaking nuts?) (circle one) in duration. After the end date of _____, the Couple's spending should remain modest. Another potentially more severe Freeze (aka The Deep Freeze") may be enacted shortly thereafter if such is required, due to backsliding or just a sheer passion for Freezes, which, when properly executed, can bring with them a feeling of real accomplishment, plus a boost in confidence, sexual performance and frequency [you have to find something to do to kill the hours that would be spent scouring websites doing pre-purchase research and ordering shoes you don't need or even like, cake mix, children's puzzles for yourself, confusing, inoperable sex toys, or your eleventh white-noise machine (keep trying, but it won't kill the voices in your head . . . they only grow louder until sweet death releases you from the torture that is this life)], as well as a strengthened overall relationship ("the Relationship").

I HAVE READ THIS AGREEMENT, I HAVE TAKEN TIME TO CONSIDER ITS IMPLICATIONS, I FULLY UNDERSTAND ITS CONTENTS (EVEN THOUGH I HAVE RAGING, UNMEDICATED ATTENTION DEFICIT DISORDER, AND SO DOES MY PARTNER), I AGREE TO ITS TERMS, AND I VOLUNTARILY SUBMIT TO ITS EXECUTION. (I also agree to seek help for my _____-purchasing addiction and to potentially have a lobotomy if advised by a reputable, licensed neurosurgeon and my shitty health insurance covers at least 50 percent of it.)

_____
Partner 1

_____
Partner 2

1.4 The Goin' Dutch Contract

Agree to share all expenses to make sure you smoke out the freeloader in the couple, if he or she exists. Sharing is caring!

_____ (Partner 1) and _____ (Partner 2), hereinafter referred to as "the Couple," hereby declare they will share all expenses in the most fair and nonsexist arrangement (includes reverse sexism; is that a thing?), split 50/50, hereinafter referred to as "Splitting" (maybe not the best term for couples, but whatever), on _____, the ____ day of the month of _____, in the year of the _____ (check the Chinese zodiac). Splitting applies to all shared bills for food, utilities, and other expenses (specified as _____, _____, _____). Chores or sex favors performed are not to be used in place of pecuniary notes (nice try, though).

Monies spent may not be tallied or compared outright in obnoxious fashion (it's human nature to be ultra-obnoxious, but especially when it comes to money), unless you are actual adults who do real budgeting, in which case you probably don't need this contract or book (still, buy extra copies for friends and enemies, and please email the authors; we need your help). If upon unbiased examination Partner 1 or Partner 2 (circle one) clearly carries the greater financial burden, he/she is permitted to bitch and moan with abandon, throw tantrums, and bitch-stare as needed (as opposed to patiently waiting for his/her partner's band to get signed or _____, yada yada yada, BS BS BS, or whatever) until the other Partner pays his or her fair share.

I HAVE READ THIS AGREEMENT, I HAVE TAKEN AS MUCH TIME AS POSSIBLE GIVEN MY ADHD (PENDING OFFICIAL MEDICAL DIAGNOSIS, WHICH SHOULDN'T BE A PROBLEM) TO CONSIDER ITS

IMPLICATIONS, I WILL NOT BE A MOOCH OR A STUPID DOORMAT,
I FULLY UNDERSTAND ITS CONTENTS, I AGREE TO ITS TERMS,
AND I VOLUNTARILY SUBMIT TO ITS EXECUTION.

_____

Partner 1

_____

Partner 2 ("2" indicates inferior status, based on
gross income)

PART 2:
Work

Wow, work sucks. It can be a uniting force and something to leverage in your relationship. For example, "I had a dream I punched your boss in the face" can be one of the most romantic things you could ever say to your significant other. However, some people pour all their time and energy into their dumb jobs, leaving little for their partners. Maybe they have a strong work ethic, or maybe they are just awkward and lame and running from something. Some folks have the opposite thing going, and they kind of need to get off their asses. So without further ado, here are some contracts about work.

☐ 2.1 THE RELAX ABOUT YOUR STUPID CAREER CONTRACT

☐ 2.2 THE STOP BEING SO RELAXED ABOUT YOUR STUPID CAREER / GET A REAL JOB / YOU'RE NOT GOING TO MAKE IT AS AN ARTIST CONTRACT

☐ 2.3 THE YOU'RE TALKING ABOUT YOUR WORK NEMESIS BUT I'M JUST HEARING A DULL BUZZING SOUND CONTRACT

☐ 2.4 THE THIS IS A BORING WORK STORY, OH WAIT, THAT'S COMPLETELY REDUNDANT CONTRACT

☐ 2.5 THE WE NEED MORE MONEY, SO GROW A SET CONTRACT

2.1 The Relax About Your Stupid Career Contract

Stop taking your career and its "trajectory" so seriously, and cease checking your work email every five fucking minutes. No one emailed you. Even if they did, no one cares, even the "author" of the email! This badass relationship is what makes life grand, not your dumb jobs! It's OK if you both get fired, evicted, and end up living under a bridge. At least you'll still have each other, and that's all that matters.

_____ (Partner 1) and _____ (Partner 2), hereinafter referred to as "the Couple," hereby declare they will not ramble on about or take their careers too seriously, hereinafter referred to as "Your Career Isn't That Important," on _____, the ____ day of the month of _____, in the year _____. Your Career Isn't That Important limits the amount a given partner can talk about their career to _____ minutes per week/month (circle one), and limits the number of times a given partner can check their work email at home to _____ times a day/week/month (circle one).

Work "emergencies" are not a special dispensation, mainly because there are no such things as work emergencies, just annoying coworkers who take themselves and their careers too seriously. The only actual work emergencies we can think of are if your office is burning down (nice!) or a colleague is expiring on the job, which, depending on that colleague, may or may not be a good thing. When one partner starts to drone on about their career or "professional future," the non-offending partner may _____ them.

This contract should remain intact in perpetuity, but if you must put time limits on it in order to reassess, Your Career Isn't That Important will expire on _____, thus totaling ____ days/weeks/months (circle one) in duration.

I HAVE READ THIS AGREEMENT, I HAVE TAKEN TIME TO CONSIDER ITS IMPLICATIONS, I FULLY UNDERSTAND ITS CONTENTS, WORK SUCKS, I AGREE TO ITS TERMS, AND I VOLUNTARILY SUBMIT TO ITS EXECUTION.

_____

Partner 1

_____

Partner 2

2.2 The Stop Being So Relaxed About Your Stupid Career / Get a Real Job / You're Not Going to Make It as an Artist Contract

Let's say one partner is a deadbeat: A "playwright." A singer-songwriter. A "dancer." An aspiring pro golfer. Cut the shit. Use this contract to lovingly crush their dreams and get them out the door and earning their keep. It was cute when you met and everything, but yeah . . . no.

_____ (Partner 1) and _____ (Partner 2), hereinafter referred to as "the Couple," agree that Partner 1 will face the music and stop chasing their boyhood/girlhood dream full-time on _____, the ___ day of the month of _____, in the year ____. Partner 1 hereby agrees to prioritize unglamorous, conventional gainful employment and let their idiotic dream of becoming a _____ die an easy, painless, and humane death.

Every person would rather be in the NBA, a working puppeteer, a celebrated high-profile blogger, or a legendary jazz-funk bassist. Literally no one dreams about being a raw-materials inventory clerk. With all due respect, Partner 1, we think you're "great" and "relatively talented," and so does Partner 2, but it's time to take the fantasy career aspirations down several notches and come to terms with the fact that you've got yourself a damn good hobby. Pride yourself on it; all most people can do is make a double-chin smartphone face and watch TV. Partner 1 agrees to get a real job doing _____ or _____, and acknowledges that when one partner is working in a frigid gray cubicle all week and the other is sleeping in and dicking around and out paying for studio time or ice time or whatever, that's pretty unbalanced, and that shit is just not going to work out.

I HAVE READ THIS AGREEMENT, I HAVE TAKEN TIME TO CONSIDER ITS IMPLICATIONS, I FULLY UNDERSTAND ITS CONTENTS, I AGREE TO ITS TERMS, I GET THAT I'M NOT THAT SPECIAL, AND I VOLUNTARILY SUBMIT TO ITS EXECUTION.

_____

Partner 1

_____

Partner 2

2.3 The You're Talking About Your Work Nemesis but I'm Just Hearing a Dull Buzzing Sound Contract

Agree to stop obsessing about a specific ass-clown coworker or your weird-as-shit HR head who doesn't blink because he read in a management book that not blinking commands respect and obedience (spoiler alert: it doesn't).

_____ (Partner 1) and _____ (Partner 2), hereinafter referred to as "the Couple," agree they will stop filling their hearts with hatred for a specific coworker and blabbing about it to no end on _____, the ____ day of the month of _____, in the year _____. The Work Nemesis Ban bars Partners from going on long, depraved, profanity-laden rants about _____ (list one or more work nemeses) and what an annoying, _____, and _____ _____ they are.

The Couple acknowledges there is nothing to gain from obsessing over the freak(s) listed above and that repeatedly ranting about them at length can start to really annoy your partner and harsh everyone's mellow. It's best not to bring that shit home. But because it's no good for your health to bottle your emotions, especially when some evil hobag throws you under the bus via email timestamp, the Partners agree to save the bulk of their exasperated, bitchy tangents for their coworkers, _____ (list name(s) of coworker(s)) or their mom*.

I HAVE READ THIS AGREEMENT, I HAVE TAKEN TIME TO CONSIDER ITS IMPLICATIONS, I FULLY UNDERSTAND ITS CONTENTS, I AGREE TO ITS TERMS, I WILL STOP LOSING IT ABOUT THAT TOOL

IN ACCOUNTING WHO IS PROBABLY ACTUALLY A REALLY NICE PERSON, AND I VOLUNTARILY SUBMIT TO ITS EXECUTION.

_____
Partner 1

_____
Partner 2

*Moms love this shit.

2.4 The This Is a Boring Work Story, Oh Wait, That's Completely Redundant Contract

Complain less about your boring work tasks and projects; no one actually understands your job anyway, nor would they want to if offered the opportunity.

_____ (Partner 1) and _____ (Partner 2), hereinafter referred to as "the Couple," agree they will generally limit the amount of time spent talking about work on _____, the ____ day of the month of _____, in the year _____. The Boring Work Story Ban prohibits Partners from telling achingly mundane and confusing stories ad nauseam that put their loved ones at risk to die of boredom and that could easily be used as an "enhanced interrogation technique," i.e., torture.

The Couple acknowledges they don't really understand the details of each other's jobs, nor do they care, and they are conscious of their Partner's boss's name, and the rest is essentially a blur. You can explain several times how you had this project that was originally supposed to be a proposal for a research grant that you ended up using as copy for a brochure that you cowrote with Jill, and how it was funny because they didn't like what . . . OMFG, no one cares; I'm falling asleep. The Couple agrees these stories are only funny to people at work who can follow them, and even then it's work and it's not actually funny.

As an alternative to long-winded blathering, some easy, courteous responses to the polite nonquestion "How was work?" include:

"Fucking terrible."

"Ew."

"Fine, whatever."

"Good."

"Not bad!"

Spontaneous twerking

_____

_____

_____

I HAVE READ THIS AGREEMENT, I HAVE TAKEN TIME TO CONSIDER ITS IMPLICATIONS, I FULLY UNDERSTAND ITS CONTENTS, I AGREE TO ITS TERMS, I WILL LIMIT THE AMOUNT TO WHICH I BLAB ABOUT WORK, ESPECIALLY WHEN MY PARTNER'S EYES ARE CLEARLY GLAZING OVER AND SLOWLY ROLLING UPWARD, AND I VOLUNTARILY SUBMIT TO ITS EXECUTION.

_____

Partner 1

_____

Partner 2

2.5 The We Need More Money, So Grow a Set Contract

Ask for raises, a promotion, take on freelance work or a special project (including but not limited to streetwalking, the oldest and most respectable profession). In other words, make more money! That's what capitalism is about . . . and we love capitalism!

_____ (Partner 1) and _____ (Partner 2), hereinafter referred to as "the Couple," declare one or more Partners must ask their respective bosses for a raise (and a promotion if desired, but do you *really* want more "responsibility"?) because the rent is too damn high on _____, the ____ day of the month of _____, in the year _____. The Partner(s) tasked with the request must complete their mission within _____ day(s)/week(s) (circle one) of signing. If your plea is not met with a clear yes or no answer, as in not a bunch of bullshit about HR and budgets and performance evaluations, the Partner(s) must ask again every ____ week(s) until they get a straight answer, for fuck's sake.

For some people, this can be a little bit of a scary undertaking. It's definitely something worth getting psyched up about, whether you're nervous or not, because if you do end up with a raise, you're going to feel like a fucking . . . well, boss, for lack of a better word. The Partners agree to act as each other's hype men in the lead-up, for example, waking your Partner up by grabbing them by the collar and shouting things like, "You got this, you brilliant jackass!" and, "You are going to go in there and fucking kill them with confidence because you are worth it, you beautiful ham sandwich!" and "_____
_____" and "_____
_____."

I HAVE READ THIS AGREEMENT, I HAVE TAKEN TIME TO CONSIDER ITS IMPLICATIONS, I FULLY UNDERSTAND ITS CONTENTS, I AGREE TO ITS TERMS, OH YEAH, WE GOT THIS, BIG MONEY, NO WHAM-MIES, AND I VOLUNTARILY SUBMIT TO ITS EXECUTION.

_____

Partner 1

_____

Partner 2

PART 3:
Sex

Sex—it's the keystone (or cornerstone? one of the stones) of a healthy relationship. Maybe it's fireworks, universes colliding in a great heavenly burst of wonderfulness. Or maybe it's just a humdrum obligation nowadays. Most likely somewhere in between. Either way, the following contracts are meant to alleviate the tension and hostility that often accompany sex and conversations about sex (yuck, just do it already). This is a good one to tear out and have displayed proudly on the fridge or corkboard (now we wish we had one of those), and probably taken down when you have visitors; on second thought, you might want to leave it up when your partner's family visits, in order to gross them out beyond recognition by trumpeting the details of your freaky (see *boring*) sex life. Ready to contractually spice things up? *Let's do it!*

☐ 3.1 THE BASIC SEX FREQUENCY CONTRACT

☐ 3.2 THE HOLIDAY SEX ROMP CONTRACT

☐ 3.3 THE FREAK-AY SEX CONTRACT

☐ 3.4 THE PORN CONTRACT

☐ 3.5 THE FANTASY THREESOME CONTRACT

☐ 3.6 THE FREE SEX PASS CONTRACT

3.1 The Basic Sex Frequency Contract

Get back to basics and get it on (includes dirty but fun acts such as kissing, cuddling, and other racy foreplay). This scalding-hot contract requires you to do the wild thing at predetermined intervals. What's sexier than that?

_____ (Partner 1) and _____ (Partner 2), hereinafter referred to as "the Couple," hereby declare they will engage in sex at least ____ times a week/month/year (!?!) (circle one), even in the face of lack of interest and/or desire. Hopefully you still have some desire. And you're probably still attracted to your Partner, at least a little, even if you've been together five, six years or more. No? Oh, come on! Just picture them back then when you really wanted them and you weren't both so old and flabby and psychologically broken. Good. Now, from that perspective, take the plunge into that bottomless abyss of mandatory sex. The Couple agrees to refrain from visible displays of lack of interest or disgust with and during the sex acts, including but not limited to sighs, eye rolling, checking/responding to emails/texts, _____, _____, and _____. Further, in executing this agreement, the couple hereby agrees to feign at least a modicum of "passion." _Just make one damn noise!_ Even if it's quite dreadful, at least you've once again demonstrated your humanitarian, Mother Teresa–like compassion for your Partner, and thus earned some bonus karma points! Win-win.

Each mandatory sex session must include ____ minutes of foreplay (it's fine to put zero if that's your MO), defined as _____
_____.

The Couple makes this vow, hereafter referred to as, simply, "Sex Agreement" (we're not that creative when it comes to this stuff) on

_____, the ___ day of the month of _____, in the year
_____.

I HAVE READ THIS AGREEMENT, I HAVE TAKEN TIME TO CONSIDER
ITS IMPLICATIONS, I FULLY UNDERSTAND ITS CONTENTS, I AGREE
TO ITS TERMS, I WILL TRY MY BEST TO PERFORM SEXUALLY
IN THE FACE OF GREAT ODDS, AND I VOLUNTARILY SUBMIT TO
ITS SEXECUTION. IS IT JUST ME OR ARE THESE ALL-CAPS SEN-
TENCES KIND OF SEXY?

_____
Partner 1

_____
Partner 2 ("2" does not indicate inferior status; actually,
in this case, it might)

3.2 The Holiday Sex Romp Contract

Never, under any circumstances, miss out on special-occasion sex, including birthdays, anniversaries, Patriots' Day (in Maine or Massachusetts, where it is a state holiday), the Final Four, *Jeopardy! Tournament of Champions,* and Wimbledon.

_____ (Partner 1) and _____ (Partner 2), hereinafter referred to as "the Couple," hereby declare they will engage in sex, hereinafter referred to as "the Sex Romp," on the holidays* (hereinafter referred to as "the Holidays") listed hereafter: _____,
_____, _____,
_____, _____, _____
_____, _____, _____
_____, _____,
_____, _____,
_____.

*For a list of obscure holidays, such as National Chocolate Covered Raisins Day (March 24), Beer Can Appreciation Day (January 24), and Lumpy Rug Day (May 3), please consult your nearest social media professional.

Couples may incorporate festive thematic elements related to the Holidays into the Sex Romp (including but definitely not limited to monocles, shamrocks, football helmets, Seder plates, aforementioned chocolate-covered raisins, etc.), which is actually kind of a cool idea.

The Couple makes this vow, hereafter referred to as "the Holiday Sex Agreement," on _____, the ____ day of the month of _____ (also know as National _____ Day), in the year _____.

I HAVE READ THIS AGREEMENT, I HAVE TAKEN TIME TO CONSIDER ITS IMPLICATIONS, I FULLY UNDERSTAND ITS CONTENTS, I AGREE TO ITS TERMS, AND I VOLUNTARILY SUBMIT TO ITS SEXECUTION.

_____

Partner 1

_____

Partner 2

3.3 The Freak-ay Sex Contract

Not doin' it and doin' it well? This contract will inspire you to put in more effort, not get tired so quickly, and even introduce some kink (anything is possible).

_____ (Partner 1) and _____ (Partner 2), hereinafter referred to as "the Potentially S&M Couple," state herein, in the eyes of the law and whoever else is watching (pervs), they will insert (pun intended) some sexy, creative, and even outlandish new wrinkles (hopefully not, but wrinkles can be sexy in the right situation . . . see, that's what we're talking about—it's getting weird).

It is clearly time to mix things up in the bedroom—or the bathroom or living room or even in the tool shed littered with rock salt where there is sometimes a raccoon napping. To get more specific, the Potentially S&M Couple agrees to try _____, _____, _____, and beep-beep-beep-beep (get it, like sensors on network TV?) in order to enhance their sexual lives and relationship. The Couple agrees to use the following safe word: _____, which means tone it down or stop, seriously.

This XXX-rated contract will expire on _____, after which the Potentially S&M Couple may choose to get more and more bold. Or if things went too far and it got too weird and now you're still awkward around each other, just take a deep breath, do some nonsexual yoga, and let it pass—it's not for you, and that's fine. Maybe just take a nice half-block stroll to the nearest Starbucks, grab a couple PSLs and then hit up the Gap afterward. That could be more up your alley, and we aren't here to judge.

I HAVE READ THIS AGREEMENT, I HAVE TAKEN TIME TO CONSIDER ITS IMPLICATIONS, I WILL TRY TO BE MORE OF A NAUGHTY FREAK

WITH MY PARTNER IN KEEPING WITH THEIR PREDILECTIONS AND SEXUAL PECCADILLOES, I FULLY UNDERSTAND ITS CONTENTS, I AGREE TO ITS TERMS, AND I VOLUNTARILY SUBMIT TO ITS SEX-ECUTION.

_____

Partner 1

_____

Partner 2 (indicates submissive status)

3.4 The Porn Contract

Porn, what a hoot, you know? It's become so ubiquitous that now it's totally acceptable, I guess, right? Like you're not a perv for having an immense porn collection? That's kinda gross and pathetic. We've regressed a bit as a society. Anyhow, this contract will help sort through unhealthy porn addictions and healthy porn usages. Better talk about it before you walk in on your partner indulging in some tentacle hentai, or something else much weirder you did not even know existed.

_____ (Partner 1) and _____ (Partner 2), hereinafter referred to as "the Couple," hereby acknowledge one or more members of the Couple probably/definitely consumes pornography (that is hopefully not of a super-disturbing variety) in a normal, healthy fashion. The Couple agrees, if they wish, to divulge all (OK, most) of their porn consumption habits to one another. Phew, don't you feel less gross/guilty now? Pervs.

The Couple acknowledges there exists a personal component to sexuality and that one or more members of the Couple likely has an embarrassing secret folder of nudie pics on his/her/their laptop, which in no way constitutes cheating, unless the Partner or Partners are colossal morons with parts of their brains missing who can't distinguish fantasy from reality (this is pretty much true).

The Couple makes this vow, hereafter referred to as, simply, "I Am OK With My Partner's Jackin' It Habits," on _____, the ____ day of the month of _____, in the year _____.

I HAVE READ THIS AGREEMENT, I HAVE TAKEN TIME TO CONSIDER ITS IMPLICATIONS, I FULLY UNDERSTAND ITS CONTENTS, I AGREE TO ITS TERMS, AND I VOLUNTARILY SUBMIT TO ITS SEXECUTION.

_____

Partner 1

_____

Partner 2

3.5 The Fantasy Threesome Contract

Threesomes . . . the ultimate goal in life, right? Nah. The ultimate goal is true happiness and bringing joy to others. But still, let's agree upon participants in fantasy threesomes, and agree to stop talking about threesomes so much because it's probably not happening. But you never know . . . So you want to go ahead and bring a third adult "human" into the bedroom (male, female, mythical gender-fluid sex nymph) because you're oh-so-bored with each other. Sure, this is going to work out.

_____ (Partner 1) and _____ (Partner 2), hereinafter referred to as "the Couple," hereby declare they will agree upon participants to participate in a fully participatory threesome. These are fantasy threesomes, the parties understand, but these fantasies can be made reality if both parties agree and have the right connections. (*Additional disclosure: As always, the authors of this "book" are not responsible for the disintegration of relationships due to scalding-hot threesomes and/or regret-filled, wishing-you-could-go-back-in-time weeping during or immediately after "the Encounter.")

The Couple will choose their partner (or partners, if one singular individual cannot be agreed upon and the couple wants to conduct two separate rendezvous for each partner's respective pleasure) and then either just fantasize about it or actually make the magic happen. Partner 1 and Partner 2 consent to engage in sexual acts in a singular encounter that includes Partner 3, _____ (i.e., that hot meter maid we saw once, Justin Bieber, an Instagram ho, Ryan Gosling, Romanian gymnastics legends, etc.). Other appointees for Partner 3 include _____ or _____. The Couple agrees to keep bragging about sex injuries sustained during the encounter to a minimum. Common injuries include getting kneed or elbowed in the face, and pulled muscles, namely adductors.

The Couple makes this vow, heretofore referred to as "the Vow" or "We're Actually Doing This Now, Right? You're Sure You're On Board . . . Really?" on _____, the ____ day of the month of _____, in the year _____.

I HAVE READ THIS AGREEMENT, I HAVE TAKEN TIME TO CONSIDER ITS IMPLICATIONS, I FULLY UNDERSTAND ITS CONTENTS, I AGREE TO ITS TERMS, I BARELY HAVE ENOUGH SEXUAL PROWESS FOR REGULAR TWO-PERSON SEX, AND I VOLUNTARILY SUBMIT TO ITS SEXECUTION.

_____

Partner 1

_____

Partner 2

_____

Partner 3 (Lol! As if you two bumbling geeks could get them to sign this! I mean, good luck and everything!)

3.6 The Free Sex Pass Contract

After a certain number of years together you might decide to give each other a free fuck pass. Ribald! Keep in mind there are usually rules involved, like only getting a free pass with a musically untalented Starbucks barista.

_____ (Partner 1) and _____ (Partner 2), hereinafter referred to as "the Couple," hereby declare to grant each other _____ (insert numerical digit) celebrity or noncelebrity (circle one) free sex pass(es). This contract, hereinafter referred to as the "I Totally Would Allow You to Seize the Moment, as in Hit That Contract," goes into effect on _____, the ____ day of the month of _____, in the year of the _____ (refer to the Chinese zodiac).

This contract dictates that each party allow their partner to engage in a singular sexual encounter with a preapproved specific regular dude or lady, or more benignly, a celebrity. The Couple may choose acquaintances they kind of have a crush on; again, Starbucks baristas are the first thing to pop into our heads. Something about Starbucks really turns us on. The coffee, the rustic countertops, the plastic-flavored but delightful Rice Krispies treats . . . it all adds up to extreme arousal for us. Also the lighting, the voluptuous, topless, erotic mermaid logo, and the green aprons . . . oh, the green aprons. Or maybe you want to go the celebrity route (less of a chance, but hey, miracles do happen); suggestions include Maria Bartiromo (see contract 1.3), Justin Timberlake, Rihanna, Edward Snowden, Oprah, Stedman, Gayle, Dr. Oz, Dr. Phil, etc.

Partner 1 bestows the gift of a free sex pass upon Partner 2. Partner 2 may have sex with the following preapproved person(s): _____ _____.

Partner 2 bestows the gift of a free sex pass upon Partner 1. Partner 1 may have sex with the following preapproved person(s): _____ _____.

This contract will expire on _____ (so act fast, if you have the balls). If you went the celeb route, the Couple acknowledges this is not your window to turn into a scary stalker and end up on the news.

Each Partner is obligated to routinely taunt the other about their Free Sex Pass selection(s), especially if said selection(s) is/are super lame, tacky, or downright goofy. This irrevocable right shall extend in perpetuity, beyond expiration of this contract.

I HAVE READ THIS AGREEMENT, I HAVE TAKEN TIME TO CONSIDER ITS IMPLICATIONS, I AM POSSIBLY A LITTLE TOO EXCITED ABOUT THIS EVEN THOUGH THERE IS A 99.9 PERCENT CHANCE IT WON'T HAPPEN, I FULLY UNDERSTAND ITS CONTENTS, I AGREE TO ITS TERMS, AND I VOLUNTARILY SUBMIT TO ITS SEXECUTION.

_____
Partner 1

_____
Partner 2

PART 4:
Grooming

One of the joys of cohabitating is getting a front-row seat to your partner's personal grooming habits. There will be quirks (and there will be blood). And because these are quirks that involve hair and teeth and pubes, it's pretty much impossible for them to be anything but weird and gross, borderline disturbing. If you haven't already, here is your chance to express the emotional damage your partner is causing you by leaving rat-sized balls of hair in the shower drain.

☐ 4.1 THE TRY TO MAINTAIN YOUR HOTNESS CONTRACT

☐ 4.2 THE THIS LITTLE PIGGY IS DISGUSTING CONTRACT

☐ 4.3 THE I ALMOST BROKE UP WITH YOU WHEN I SAW YOUR
BATHROOM FOR THE FIRST TIME CONTRACT

☐ 4.4 THE GAS CONTROL CONTRACT

4.1 The Try to Maintain Your Hotness Contract

Agree to maintain baseline attractiveness and not let yourself totally go to hell—attempt to exercise a little, even spruce up your look from time to time, and maybe don't immediately reach for the sweatpants every time you step inside the damn house (no pants is fine).

_____ (Partner 1) and _____ (Partner 2), hereinafter referred to as "the Couple," declare with stoic determination that they will try to stay somewhat attractive, hereinafter referred to as "the Attractiveness Clause," on _____, the ____ day of the month of _____, in the year of our Lord / the devil (for all you Satan worshipers; we know you're out there and this book would appeal to you) _____. The Attractiveness Clause prohibits both partners from gaining _____ pounds/kilos (circle one), losing _____ pounds, not grooming _____, _____ properly, and wearing _____, _____, or _____ all the fucking time.

This is not to suggest that each Partner must retain fembot-cyber-ho or Joe Manganiello levels of babedom, which requires tons of time, money, maintenance, superficiality, and lasers, but that each Partner's hotness evolves appropriately over time and there are no drastic, disturbing declines (which would probably signal some level of clinical depression, so check into that, would you?). Additionally, each Partner is required to wear something super-hot at least _____ times a week/month/year as a reminder that their Partner will still momentarily look away from their phone to check them out and compliment them.

I HAVE READ THIS AGREEMENT, I HAVE TAKEN TIME TO CONSIDER ITS IMPLICATIONS, I FULLY UNDERSTAND ITS CONTENTS, I AGREE

TO ITS TERMS, I WILL TRY TO REMAIN KINDA HOT, AND I VOLUN-
TARILY SUBMIT TO ITS EXECUTION.

_____

Scalding Hot Partner 1

_____

Scalding Hot Partner 2

4.2 The This Little Piggy Is Disgusting Contract

Set restrictions on fingernail and toenail length and clippings, nose hair length and clippings, management of rogue back hairs and other unwanted body hair, as well as other general grooming rules.

_____ (Partner 1) and _____ (Partner 2), hereinafter referred to as "the Couple," declare they will make their best efforts to uphold consistent standards in their respective hygiene habits, hereinafter referred to as "I Will Only Be as Gross as Is OK With You, My Dear," on _____, the ____ day of the month of _____, in the year of our Neat Freak Lord _____.

This contract prohibits Partners from lapsing into a near-feral state in terms of unkempt head, facial, nipple, and body hair, requiring regular maintenance of agreed-upon lengths (give or take a few millimeters) for nose/ear hair, brows, chest/back hair, pits, pubes, legs, and that weird long hair that grows out of Partner 1/2's (circle one or both) _____.

Partners permit / do not permit (circle one) one another to use each other's grooming tools (tweezers, scissors, razors, waxes, chainsaws). For safety purposes, and in the interest of preserving bed linens and rugs/carpeting, Partners must keep toenails at a reasonable length, and of course clippings should be properly disposed of, i.e., not left on a coffee table or _____.

The authors prefer not to go into zit-popping territory (although feel free to add your own addendum), but generally each Partner agrees not to offend the other in this realm. Let's face it, we all need to just shut that down.

Upon signing, this contract exists in perpetuity, especially since as you get older you get hairier and hairier. And your nose gets bigger. Someone kill me.

I HAVE READ THIS AGREEMENT, I HAVE TAKEN TIME TO CONSIDER ITS IMPLICATIONS, I FULLY UNDERSTAND ITS CONTENTS, I AGREE TO ITS TERMS, I WILL TRY MY BEST NOT TO TURN INTO COUSIN IT EVEN THOUGH I HAVE AN UNREGULATED HORMONE PROBLEM, AND I VOLUNTARILY SUBMIT TO ITS EXECUTION.

_____
Partner 1

_____
Partner 2

4.3 The I Almost Broke Up with You When I Saw Your Bathroom for the First Time Contract

Set rules and responsibilities for where it all goes down. There has to be something out there that stops you from peeing on the toilet seat! What if we chopped off your ding-dong (that's a contract for another time)? You'd still do it, wouldn't you? Turn on the damn light if you have bad aim!

_____ (Partner 1) and _____ (Partner 2), hereinafter referred to as "the Couple," hereby declare they will enact rules for regular, evolved human-standard bathroom behaviors and maintenance, hereinafter referred to as the "Let's Not Have a Bus Station Bathroom Act," on _____, the ____ day of the month of _____, in the year _____.

This Act enlists each Partner to take meaningful action in routinely correcting their lazy and/or gross bathroom habits. These can include but are not limited to: not replenishing the TP; replenishing the TP but failing to put the new roll on the holder; loading the TP on the holder but failing to put it on the right way; toilet seat up/down shenanigans (*classic!*); sprinkling whilst tinkling; hair, hair, hair, and hairballs everywhere; plain idiotic and/or passive-aggressive means of dispensing toothpaste; globs of toothpaste left in the sink because we're all just going to die anyway; etc. and so on.

Partner 1 solemnly swears to correct the following annoying and/or gross bathroom habits: _____
_____
_____
_____.

Partner 2 solemnly swears to correct the following annoying and/or gross bathroom habits: _____

_____

_____

_____

The Let's Not Have a Bus Station Bathroom Act expires upon disbandment of the Couple because, understandably, one of you is just too gross to be around on a daily basis.

I HAVE READ THIS AGREEMENT, I HAVE TAKEN TIME TO CONSIDER ITS IMPLICATIONS, I FULLY UNDERSTAND ITS CONTENTS, I AGREE TO ITS TERMS, I AM NOT READING THIS ON THE TOILET, AND I VOLUNTARILY SUBMIT TO ITS EXECUTION.

_____
Partner 1

_____
Partner 2 (here, "2" indicates inferior status and poo)

4.4 The Gas Control Contract

Your relationship is at the point where you're comfortable performing certain normal healthy bodily functions in front of one another. That's really great! But . . . you know . . . don't be gross. Limit it, eliminate it, or just leave the room!

_____ (Fartner 1) and _____ (Fartner 2), hereinafter referred to as "the Couple," declare with clarity and determination that they will be gracious and mindful in the flatulence department on _____, the ____ day of the month of _____, in the year _____. The Gas Control Contract bars Partners from rude displays of gas passing such as ripping a huge fart in the middle of a fight, letting out a butt explosion in the middle of someone's sincere stress rant or amazing story, loud operatic burping as a response to a question, ____ _____, _____, and _____.

Odds are, one of you guys is a total gas factory, likely the cuter, more innocent-looking one. Just because you can let out an impressive fart or burp at a moment's notice, there is simply no need to wield this lethal skill for sport. Each Partner agrees to say "Excuse me" or _____ upon launching an air biscuit, floating a fish oil burp, etc. To remove any scary Dutch oven–style scenarios, locations where farting and/or severe burping is not permitted under any circumstances include: in bed, during mealtimes, in elevators, _____, _____, and _____.

I HAVE READ THIS AGREEMENT, I HAVE TAKEN TIME TO CONSIDER ITS IMPLICATIONS, I FULLY UNDERSTAND ITS CONTENTS, I AGREE

TO ITS TERMS, I AM CURRENTLY HOLDING IN A HUGE FART, AND I VOLUNTARILY SUBMIT TO ITS EXECUTION.

_____

Fartner 1

_____

Fartner 2

PART 5:

Matters of Taste

It's the rare individual who can admit they have terrible taste. We're talking about people who just don't get it—what looks good, what's cool, what isn't lame—and can acknowledge that fact. Your partner is probably not one of these wise individuals. He or she is probably one of the 99 percent who think their taste and their opinions on matters of taste are actually superior or even relevant. But the truth is, one of you has better taste than the other in certain areas (i.e., home decor, music, film, food, fashion, personal style, etc.). Sort it out and be prepared to agree to disagree, or simply submit to the pushier, more annoying partner if you haven't already. Sign away and enjoy your new and improved stylish life!

☐ 5.1 THE HOME DECOR CONTRACT

☐ 5.2 THE MUSIC NERD / DJ CONTRACT

☐ 5.3 THE WARDROBE AND STYLE CONTRACT

☐ 5.4 THE "OH, UM, THANKS . . . YOU REALLY SHOULDN'T HAVE" CONTRACT

5.1 The Home Decor Contract

Put the hammer *down!* Decide which one of you has a better design sense when it comes to home decorating, and let them make 99 percent of the decisions in this area. Or if you both suck, just ban the one who sucks more.

_____ (Partner 1) and _____ (Partner 2), hereinafter referred to as "the Couple," declare they will bar the partner with inferior decorating taste (referred to as "Tasteless, Trash-Can Partner") from making decisions about home decor, hereinafter referred to as "the Decor Ban," on _____, the ____ day of the month of _____, in the year of the devil _____.

The Decor Ban prohibits the Tasteless, Trash-Can Partner from making decisions about home decor or participating in the discussion, even in an abstract fashion. In other words, the Tasteless, Trash-Can Partner can have absolutely *zero* input in the process of decorating your shared living space, regardless (or perhaps because) of how much HGTV they watch. As an alternative to offering any comments whatsoever about decor, he/she is welcome to be silent and go read a book in the corner or the attic crawlspace. Beat it. I mean, you're adorable, *love you!* Furthermore, we hereby declare the Tasteless, Trash-Can Partner may not make any *purchases* in the realm of home decor. While this ban is in effect, the Tasteless, Trash-Can Partner may only purchase food items to sustain him-/herself and personal-care products (subject to approval from the less trashy partner). Otherwise, they can and should be completely shut down with regard to garbage pail opinions and purchases.

The Decor Ban will expire on _____, thus totaling ____ days/weeks/months (circle one) in duration.

I HAVE READ THIS AGREEMENT, I HAVE TAKEN TIME TO CONSIDER ITS IMPLICATIONS, I FULLY UNDERSTAND ITS CONTENTS, I AGREE TO ITS TERMS, AND I VOLUNTARILY SUBMIT TO ITS EXECUTION (AND I AGREE TO BEING VIDEOTAPED AS I SAY "I AM A TACKY BITCH" FOR THE OFFICIAL RECORD, AKA EXHIBIT A).

_____

Partner 1

_____

Partner 2 ("2" definitely indicates inferior status here; try to improve yourself, goddamn it)

5.2 The Music Nerd / DJ Contract

This sweet little contract allows the partner with superior taste in music to make the large majority of decisions regarding music choices—in the car, at home, at the beach, or on the slopes *shooshing* away.

_____ (Partner 1) and _____ (Partner 2), hereinafter referred to as "the Couple," hereby agree to appoint _____ (Partner's name) to serve a life tenure as the couple's Honorable Disc Jockey (hereafter referred to as "the DJ"—creative, we know).

The DJ is responsible for supplying appropriate, good-sounding shit for the Couple in a variety of settings, with absolutely no fanfare or braggadocio-type behavior, saving any and all armchair A&R or Rock Historian commentary for their college friends. Furthermore, this honor bestowed upon the DJ shall be accepted coolly, with no further mention of their hard-earned and deeply admirable knowing-about-and-liking-cool-shit achievements, such as _____ _____, _____, _____ _____, _____, and _____ _____ (i.e., they *prefer* '80s Dylan, or they were once at a party at this recording studio with Benny Blanco, who is like this huge producer that you probably don't even know about, but whatever . . .).

The DJ can play _____ (number) requests made by the "non-DJ" Partner per day/week/month (circle one) without protest, and acknowledges that the "non-DJ" would like a break from jamming out all the damn time and that it is appropriate to occasionally vibe out on the white-noise machine.

The DJ may choose to resign at any time, and is subject to removal under extreme circumstances (for example, their taste becomes so hyperevolved and sophisticated that it begins to transcend time and space and thus severely minimizes "the Relationship," or they start revisiting nü metal unironically). Optional: The appointee must retire from service at the age of _____.

I HAVE REMOVED MY EXPENSIVE EARBUDS AND READ THE ABOVE AGREEMENT, I HAVE TAKEN TIME TO CONSIDER ITS IMPLICATIONS, I FULLY UNDERSTAND ITS CONTENTS, I AGREE TO ITS TERMS, AND I VOLUNTARILY SUBMIT TO ITS EXECUTION.

_____

Partner 1

_____

Partner 2 ("2" definitely indicates inferior status here; step it up!)

5.3 The Wardrobe and Style Contract

Please try to avoid clothes that make you look clinically depressed and other such style faux pas. Well, any look can be pulled off if you know what youre doing. Just don't offend your partner with your tatters.

_____ (Partner 1) and _____ (Partner 2), hereinafter referred to as "the Couple," hereby declare they will permanently ban the following listed items from their respective wardrobes on _____, the ____ day of the month of _____, in the year _____. Examples of ban-able "garments" include: that sack you call a shirt that makes you look like you live under a bridge, those vomit-colored shorts, underwear from any Bush administration, malodorous polyester vintage "pieces," parachute pants that make your butt disappear, that grossly oversized cardigan ("I can't see your body! Where are you? I miss you!"), and that shirt you wear to bed that looks like it has mold growing on it.

Partner 1, without protest, must discard, safely burn (ideally), bury, or quarantine the following items: _____, _____, and _____.

Partner 2, without protest, must discard, safely burn (ideally), bury, or quarantine the following items: _____, _____, and _____.

If the couple cannot agree to discard items and there exists a serious rift in fashion sensibilities, the authors suggest the couple dress in matching outfits every day for decades, à la Donald Featherstone (inventor of the plastic lawn flamingo) and his wife, Nancy. It sounds like you guys are really sweating the small stuff and could learn a great deal from them.

This contract exists in perpetuity.

I HAVE READ THIS AGREEMENT, I HAVE TAKEN TIME TO CONSIDER ITS IMPLICATIONS, I FULLY UNDERSTAND ITS CONTENTS, I WILL TOTALLY GET RID OF THESE BELOVED TREASURES THAT FILL ME WITH COMFORT AND JOY, I AM NOT CROSSING MY FINGERS BEHIND MY BACK, I AGREE TO ITS TERMS, AND I VOLUNTARILY SUBMIT TO ITS EXECUTION.

_____
Partner 1

_____
Partner 2

5.4 The "Oh, Um, Thanks . . . You Really Shouldn't Have" Contract

Agree not to exchange gifts for the holidays (or only with advance approval from the recipient), or else things might get weird and/ or testy: "That's my Christmas present? A pen, a lighter, and an unwrapped bull's-eye caramel? Why does this look suspiciously similar to the contents of a glove compartment?"

_____ (Partner 1) and _____ (Partner 2), hereinafter referred to as "the Couple," hereby declare they will put a temporary ban on mutual holiday gift-giving, hereinafter referred to as the "Useless Crap Ban," on _____, the ____ day of the month of _____, in the year _____ (or Mayan calendar equivalent), with the exception of _____ (list *one* holiday, if desired).

The couple agrees most holidays exist predominantly to stimulate commerce (or worse, to make you spend time with your family, or even worse, to do "religious stuff") and that they don't need to buy one another dumb, useless presents 'cause they're supposed to on a certain day. Besides, who has time to buy gifts, much less come up with thoughtful ones when there are phones to be stared at and drooled upon? Spontaneous gift-giving is permitted (yeah, that's gonna happen). Any nonspontaneous holiday-related gifts must be purchased with prior written or verbal consent from the recipient. This Agreement does not permit one or more Partners to be Grinch-y d-bags, nor does it bar them from getting into the sprit of a given season or holiday if they fucking feel like it.

The Useless Crap Ban will expire on _____, thus totaling ____ days/weeks/months (circle one) in duration.

I HAVE READ THIS AGREEMENT, I HAVE TAKEN TIME TO CONSIDER ITS IMPLICATIONS, I FULLY UNDERSTAND ITS CONTENTS, I AGREE TO ITS TERMS, I VOLUNTARILY SUBMIT TO ITS EXECUTION, AND I . . . WAIT . . . WAIT, WHERE THE HELL IS MY VALENTINE'S DAY PRESENT?! I DIDN'T *ACTUALLY* MEAN NOT TO GET ME SOMETHING FOR V-DAY! LOL, JUST KIDDING!

_____

Partner 1

_____

Partner 2

PART 6:

Health and Wellness

While your partner may mostly nag you just to be an annoying little shit, they can also nag you in ways that can actually improve your health and well-being, such as forcing you to take vitamins, monitoring your quiet descent into alcoholism, or telling you to get off your fat ass and exercise. Couples get happy and plump together, but that's a little depressing, and have you filled out contract 4.1? You guys are supposed to be keeping it tight! Fill out these contracts and reach your full potential as a fit, healthy couple. That sounds a little obnoxious, but you get the idea.

☐ 6.1 THE FOOD RESTRICTIONS CONTRACT

☐ 6.2 THE DO YOU HAVE ANYTHING THAT'S VEGAN, GLUTEN-FREE, AND LOW IN SUGAR? CONTRACT

☐ 6.3 THE LET'S AVOID AN INTERVENTION CONTRACT

☐ 6.4 THE TOXIN FREEZE CONTRACT, OR, THE YOU'RE REMINDING ME OF KEITH RICHARDS MINUS THE QUALITY RIFFS (NEWS FLASH: YOUR RIFFS BLOW) CONTRACT

☐ 6.5 THE THAT COUGH SOUNDS FAKE CONTRACT

☐ 6.6 THE ONE, TWO, THREE, FOUR . . . GO WORK OUT BY YOURSELF! CONTRACT

☐ 6.7 THE IF I DON'T GET A GOOD NIGHT'S SLEEP, I'M GOING TO KILL MYSELF AND THEN YOU CONTRACT

6.1 The Food Restrictions Contract

Agree to go on a health-food kick, with some junk food allowances—but also agree that juice cleanses are never acceptable! Nor is talking in detail about your irritable bowel(s), tapeworm, parasite, or other unpleasant digestive situations.

_____ (Partner 1) and _____ (Partner 2), hereinafter referred to as "the Couple," declare they will go on a well-researched (not reckless) health kick on _____, the ____ day of the month of _____, in the year _____. The Let's Not Be Squishy Tubs of Lard Contract prohibits Partners from eating the following junk (here you are to actually name the crappy foods and fast food joints you regularly indulge in, not random stuff you never eat anyway): _____, _____, _____, _____, _____, _____, and _____. Examples include candy, cookies, soda, juice, McSlut's, Dunkin', or if you want to be fancy, complex carbs and refined sugars or whatever.

For reference, some healthy (more or less) things you guys like to eat include: _____
_____
_____
_____
_____ .

The Couple may opt to have a weekly cheat day (or meal, if you're hardcore) on _____, during which Partners may eat whatever the hell they want. This is not a ticket to binge-eat; it's just a day to have a can of Coke and some ice cream and enjoy the living hell out of it.

This contract expires on the ____ day of the month of _____, in the year _____. See how it goes, though; you may just want to extend it. Or maybe life without pastries every couple days isn't all that doable. We understand.

I HAVE READ THIS AGREEMENT, I HAVE TAKEN TIME TO CONSIDER ITS IMPLICATIONS, I FULLY UNDERSTAND ITS CONTENTS, I AGREE TO ITS TERMS, BUT I AM SUDDENLY CRAVING OREOS, DAMN, AND I VOLUNTARILY SUBMIT TO ITS EXECUTION.

_____
Partner 1

_____
Partner 2

6.2 The Do You Have Anything That's Vegan, Gluten-Free, and Low in Sugar? Contract

Agree that you will be chill and not judge each other's stupid diet choices no matter if you're vegan / vegetarian / paleo / keto / gluten-free or follow an otherwise annoying, nonsensical diet.

_____ (Partner 1) and _____ (Partner 2), hereinafter referred to as "the Couple," declare they will respect one another's obnoxious self-imposed dietary restrictions on _____, the ___ day of the month of _____, in the year _____. The Oh My God How Did I Ever Convince Myself That It Was OK to Date a Vegan? Contract limits Partners from ragging on each other over one partner's completely nonessential dietary restrictions, which include _____ _____, i.e., they refuse to eat animal products, refined sugars, or they have a mythical, illusory gluten intolerance, etc.

In lieu of loud sighing and face-covering, especially in restaurants during embarrassing waitstaff interrogation sessions over soup bases, Partners will _____ (describe coping mechanism(s) here). In turn, Partners must not constantly broadcast their diet choices / fad adherences, especially if motivated by digestive repercussions and/or Gwyneth Paltrow, and will try to be less annoying in restaurants and in general, to the very best of their pathetic abilities.

This contract expires on the ___ day of the month of _____, in the year _____, upon which diet choices may be reevaluated, because nutrition science and dieting trends have probably changed, and no one likes conventional wisdom because it's boring. Sad!

I HAVE READ THIS AGREEMENT, I HAVE TAKEN TIME TO CONSIDER ITS IMPLICATIONS, I FULLY UNDERSTAND ITS CONTENTS, I AGREE TO ITS TERMS, IS THIS BOOK PRINTED WITH SOY-BASED INKS, AND IF SO, IS IT NON-GMO? I MEAN I'M NOT GOING TO EAT IT BUT, LIKE, I'M JUST CURIOUS, AND I VOLUNTARILY SUBMIT TO ITS EXECUTION.

_____

Partner 1

_____

Partner 2

6.3 The Let's Avoid an Intervention Contract

Set alcohol/drug consumption limitations for yourselves. It's easy enough to lose your job, your friends, and your dignity without the help of alcohol. Add the Internet to that equation and things get really messy. At the next office party, you can let some other drunk person stick their hand in the CFO's while they're talking for once.

_____ (Partner 1) and _____ (Partner 2), hereinafter referred to as "the Couple," declare they will enact the following restrictions on drug and alcohol intake on _____, the ____ day of the month of _____, in the year _____.

If the Couple manages to drink in moderation all the time, and only over-indulges once in a blue moon (all things in moderation, including moderation), they may agree to keep up the good work. We're impressed. Alternately, if the Couple finds themselves in sloppy straits due to excessive drinking by one or more Partners, the following restrictions apply:

• Day drinking must always be capped at _____ drinks per day-drinking extravaganza.

• At a fancy dinner (home or out), each Partner may consume between _____ and ____ alcoholic beverages, assuming neither partner will be driving at any point.

• At a special event, including work parties and weddings, each Partner may consume between _____ and _____alcoholic beverages, assuming neither partner will be driving at any point.

• For a nightcap, _____ drink(s) is/are permitted, assuming no more than ____ drink(s) has/have already been imbibed earlier in the evening.

As for getting blunted, Partner 1 will limit pot smoking to _____ times per day/week/month/year/decade (circle one) and Partner 2 will limit pot smoking to _____ times per day/week/month/year/decade (circle one).

The Let's Avoid an Intervention Contract will expire on _____, thus totaling _____ days/weeks/months (circle one) in duration.

I HAVE READ THIS AGREEMENT, I HAVE TAKEN TIME TO CONSIDER ITS IMPLICATIONS, I FULLY UNDERSTAND ITS CONTENTS, I AGREE TO ITS TERMS, I MAM DRUNNIK, AND I VOLUNTARILY SUBMIT TO ITS EXECUTION.

_____
Partner 1

_____
Partner 2

6.4 The Toxin Freeze Contract, or, the You're Reminding Me of Keith Richards Minus the Quality Riffs (News Flash: Your Riffs Blow) Contract

Set periods of complete abstinence. (As Keith Richards once mumbled in the midst of a blackout, "Anything is possible.")

_____ (Partner 1) and _____ (Partner 2), hereinafter referred to as "the Couple," declare they will go on insane, extreme, probably-useless-in-the-long-run periods of abstinence on _____, the ____ day of the month of _____, in the year _____. The Toxin Freeze temporarily bans Partners from indulging in the following substances: _____

_____

(i.e., caffeine, cigarettes, smack, meth, weed, Twinkies, Twitter, Internet comments sections, etc.).

The Freeze will expire on _____, thus totaling ____ days/weeks/months (months? Again, are you freaking nuts?) (circle one) in duration. The Couple will likely be plagued by night sweats, withdrawal headaches, and overwhelming irritability and despair; however, they agree to be as nice to each other as possible, and will kindly remind each other that this Freeze is literally reversing time and taking years off their gorgeous faces. That is, if they aren't wincing with a caffeine withdrawal–induced migraine whilst banging their head on a desk.

I HAVE READ THIS AGREEMENT, I HAVE TAKEN TIME TO CONSIDER ITS IMPLICATIONS, I FULLY UNDERSTAND ITS CONTENTS, I AGREE TO ITS TERMS, I AM NOT COVERTLY MAINLINING ESPRESSO, AND I VOLUNTARILY SUBMIT TO ITS EXECUTION.

_____
Partner 1

_____
Partner 2

6.5 The That Cough Sounds Fake Contract

Be nice and accommodating when your partner is sick. On the other hand, create protections against the "sick" individual milking it (i.e., whining, moaning, and generally acting like a little baby bitch).

_____ (Partner 1) and _____ (Partner 2), hereinafter referred to as "the Couple," hereby declare they will give sympathy and assistance where it is due in the case of their Partner's illness, showing their Partner just how much they love and cherish them when their Partner is down and out. It's symbolic of the deep devotion the Couple feels for each other, as well as providing a practical service (fetching saltines, ice water, chilled pickle juice, turning up/down the white-noise machine, _____, and _____). Yet, and this is a big _yet_, each Partner hereby declares that with proper evidence (you have to be at least 95 percent sure there are some hijinks going on or else things could get ugly . . . we know from experience), the offending Partner can be called out for faking, significantly exaggerating, and/ or hamming up their "illness" in order to get attention / be waited on / receive neck rubs, couch-side cool-cloth service, butt rubs ("lower, lower, lower . . .") _____, _____, and _____.

If the "ill" Partner is in fact ill and is not being melodramatic or making up the illness altogether (making up an illness is truly deranged; we're not ten anymore—put the book down if you are ten or younger, but thanks for reading—trying to get out of school . . . although we are often trying to get out of going to work, which is perfectly natural and mature) and this individual is called out for faking, fireworks will ensue. Be sure the "ill" Partner is faking or exaggerating before you start berating them and calling them a "total pussy."

This naturally leads to the second part of the contract, which comes from the perspective of the "sick" individual. Each Partner hereby proclaims that they will not fake illnesses, exaggerate illnesses, or act like a big sickly pathetic mess (even when sick) to garner sympathy and/or make your partner act as a nurse/waitperson/_____/ mommy/daddy figure because you genuinely enjoy being babied and acting sick is a way to revel in this unseemly proclivity.

Hey, some illnesses can't be avoided, and we all love to miss work, but this contract also encourages the Couple to stay healthy. *Huh?!* Why not eat right, sleep at least eight hours a night, and just be positive overall (stress has been shown to increase . . . blah, blah, blah)? Oh, that's right, because doing everything perfectly sucks and is super-annoying! This Stop Faking agreement shall expire on _____.

I HAVE READ THIS AGREEMENT, I HAVE TAKEN TIME TO CONSIDER ITS IMPLICATIONS, I WILL NOT CURL UP IN THE FETAL POSITION AND MOAN UNLESS I AM DYING, I AGREE TO ITS TERMS, AND I VOLUNTARILY SUBMIT TO ITS EXECUTION.

_____
Partner 1

_____
Partner 2

6.6 The One, Two, Three, Four . . . Go Work Out by Yourself! Contract

Agree not to work out together or horn in on each other's fitness regimens. Also relax about hot yoga, CrossFit, Insanity, SoulCycle, or other trendy fitness crazes, and don't force it on your partner. If you guys work out together and love it . . . well, this one ain't for you. Move it along.

_____ (Partner 1) and _____ (Partner 2), hereinafter referred to as "the Couple," declare they will respect each other's fitness regimens, or lack thereof, on _____, the ____ day of the month of _____, in the year _____. This contract prohibits Partners from horning in on each other's workouts unless explicitly invited. It also prohibits Partners from forcing each other to participate in their cult/workout of choice, whether it be CrossFit, SoulCycle, Orangetheory or, in this case, _____, in spite of constant, wild proselytizing and many imbibed gallons of Kool-Aid.

For many people, working out is something you do alone or with a pal. It's nice "me" time, or away-from-your-significant-other time. The Couple acknowledges that this may be a sweet little place for a boundary in the Relationship. Do you really want to be that stock-photo couple, running and smiling together like deranged Martin O'Malley supporters? Also, didn't you go for a run together when you first started dating, and though you tried your best to impress, someone faked a leg cramp and had to take a little "break" to "stretch," as in barf behind some bushes? Let's not go through that again. Not good "optics" as they say.

When it comes to forcing your Partner to work out with you, no means no! How are you going to feel when they re-tear a glute doing too-heavy back squats (still trying to impress) and it's all your fault? There are other ways to encourage your partner to exercise on their own time, such as changing the Wi-Fi password until they join a gym and actually go, or _____

_____.

I HAVE READ THIS AGREEMENT, I HAVE TAKEN TIME TO CONSIDER ITS IMPLICATIONS, I FULLY UNDERSTAND ITS CONTENTS, I AGREE TO ITS TERMS, I WILL KEEP MY PARKOUR OBSESSION TO MY-SELF AND NOT CLING TO IT AS MY ALL-CONSUMING IDENTITY, AND I VOLUNTARILY SUBMIT TO ITS EXECUTION.

_____
Partner 1

_____
Partner 2

6.7 The If I Don't Get a Good Night's Sleep, I'm Going to Kill Myself and Then You Contract

Snoring. Jimmy legs. Aggressive cuddling. Sheet and cover hogging. Sleep farting. Sleep belching. Sleep winking. Nipple tracing. Making a ruckus with plastic and paper bags for no apparent reason. There are myriad ways your partner can fuck up your sleep, and this makes you a nightmare to be around the following day(s).

_____ (Partner 1) and _____ (Partner 2), hereinafter referred to as "the Couple," declare they will take every possible measure to ensure their Partner gets their beauty rest on _____, the ____ day of the month of _____, in the year _____. Beauty rest, or a good night's sleep, is defined as between _____ and _____ hours of sleep on most nights, or _____ nights per week if you want to get specific. This contract ensures all measures are taken to prevent sleep disturbances, with the failsafe being sleeping in separate beds (or at least the offending partner taking a night or two on the couch; aka a timeout). We know sleeping in separate beds is hard-core, but it is better than doing life at a Supermax prison in Colorado for murder.

At or just before bedtime, Partners may not _____, _____, _____, and _____ (examples include starting fights, slamming doors, coming to bed late and futzing about with phone brightness on full blast, etc.). During sleep, each Partner will attempt, to the best of their unconscious abilities, to be polite, non-violent, quiet bedfellows, and will work to remedy their terrible habits of _____ (Partner 1) and _____ (Partner 2) while they're sleeping.

Partners agree on a weekday or daily (circle one) "lights-out" time of _____. Lights-out time means the Couple is in bed or at least in the bedroom winding down, with all lights out except bedside lamps(s) and reading lamps; electronic devices are off or asleep, except the white-noise machine (crank it up!), vibes are chill and low-key (unless it's time for preplanned sex, hubba hubba), _____ _____, and _____.

If one Partner has severe, potentially dangerous sleep problems that make it especially difficult for their partner to sleep, such as insomnia or sleep dancing, they agree to seek treatment at one of those weird sleep center places, where who knows what the hell happens.

I HAVE READ THIS AGREEMENT, I HAVE TAKEN TIME TO CONSIDER ITS IMPLICATIONS, I FULLY UNDERSTAND ITS CONTENTS, I AGREE TO ITS TERMS, I WILL STOP ACTING LIKE A ROCKETTE IN THE SHEETS (AND NOT IN A GOOD WAY), AND I VOLUNTARILY SUBMIT TO ITS EXECUTION.

_____
Partner 1

_____
Partner 2

PART 7

Food and Dining

What should we have for dinner? The question strikes fear into the hearts of couples around the globe. From health kicks to 7-Eleven dinners, your culinary adventures can be the best experiences and come with the worst fights. Before one of you bursts into a hangry fit of rage, remember these contracts are here to help you with this relentless struggle of what to stuff your greedy faces with each day. And you are goddamn lucky to have each other to eat with, because for one thing, cooking for one person is a pain in the ass.

☐ 7.1 THE TAKEOUT BAN

☐ 7.2 THE SKIP FIGHTING OVER WHERE TO EAT AND GO
    DIRECTLY TO OLIVE GARDEN CONTRACT

☐ 7.3 THE WOW, YOUR COOKING TASTES JUST LIKE
    GORDON RAMSEY'S CONTRACT

☐ 7.4 THE LET'S MAKE BELIEVE IT'S 1957 AND SIT AT
    THE FUCKING TABLE CONTRACT

☐ 7.5 THE GROW UP AND EAT YOUR DAMN
    VEGETABLES CONTRACT

7.1 The Takeout Ban

Like a spending freeze but for ordering in, fatties. Put limits on your food-related "cash burn." You will have to set down the phone, clear the cobwebs off your stove, and cook something. Stop taking the special miracle of delivery via app for granted! Just boil some water, throw in some ramen, and save thirty to forty dollars. Everyone knows ramen has all the vitamins and nutrients you need to be robust and sexually potent. Just pay the extra fifteen cents for the "fancy" kind, you cheap sons of bitches.

_____ (Partner 1) and _____ (Partner 2), hereinafter referred to as "the Couple," hereby declare they will stop being so lazy and using up potential retirement/RV/camper money just so they don't have to get off their asses and cook or make a quick trip to the grocery store. We know that if you are reading this book you need help and are probably not rich, and that's OK. That's where we're at too, so this is a simple way to both save money and become healthier! Don't fight it; just become a better fucking person. Saving, let's say, sixty to eighty dollars a month by not ordering food all the goddamn time will help you be less poor. We have done extensive research, and this is 100 percent true*. Unless, of course, you cook with a ton of vanilla beans, oysters, Parmesan, and almond butter concurrently, which just sounds gross.

The Couple hereby declares they will limit their ordering of delivery/takeout to _____ times per month / fiscal quarter (circle one). This should make your life better (or make you angrier but slightly less poor) and also make the occasions when you do order in more special. Think of how good those cheap, cold tacos from down the street will taste if you deprive yourself for a few weeks!

The Couple makes this vow on _____, the ____ day of the month of _____, in the enriching, health-filled, improving-yourself-by-taking-baby-steps year _____.

I HAVE READ THIS AGREEMENT, I HAVE TAKEN TIME TO CONSIDER ITS IMPLICATIONS, I FULLY UNDERSTAND ITS CONTENTS, I AGREE TO ITS TERMS, THE INDIAN RESTAURANT DOWN THE STREET IS OVERPRICED AND OVERRATED (YOU KNOW SOME OF THOSE YELP REVIEWS ARE FAKE), AND I VOLUNTARILY SUBMIT TO ITS EXECUTION.

_____
Partner 1

_____
Partner 2

*We have not done any research and have no evidence to support this claim.

7.2 The Skip Fighting Over Where to Eat and Go Directly to Olive Garden Contract

Ban dining indecisiveness for good by agreeing (or threatening yourselves, as the case may be) to eat at America's favorite authentic Italian restaurant. Because who doesn't love bottomless salad and breadsticks? And the occasional rat running across the room for said breadsticks that fall to the floor?

_____ (Partner 1) and _____ (Partner 2), hereinafter referred to as "the Couple," hereby declare if they are unable to just freaking make a decision and agree on a place to dine for lunch or dinner they, by default, must (willingly or forcibly) make themselves eat at Cracker Barrel, Ruby Tuesday, Golden Corral, Sizzler, Olive Garden (circle one), or _____. From the time the decision to go out to eat has been made, the Couple is allowed between _____ and _____ minutes/seconds (circle one) to come to a bipartisan, irreversible decision on somewhere to eat. If they fail to do so, they must immediately make a beeline for the nearest chain as indicated earlier in this paragraph.

This contract remains in effect while traveling as well as at home. For quick, unnerving reference, the Couple's nearest Olive Garden Italian Restaurant (or comparable corporate slop trough) is located at _____ _____.

The Couple may not back out, even if church or some kind of large children's sporting event just let out, even if they are near Times Square, or even if there's a crazy long wait. They may not back out, even if one or both Partners claim to be "suddenly not feeling that well" or "not really that hungry anymore." They must forge ahead through unending heaps of salad, infinite onslaughts of pale, doughy batons, and shallow swaths of dense, beany soups, while silently processing their remorse before sinking into a deep carb-induced depression. All that said, dining at tacky restaurant chains, ironically or unironically, is good fun. So we're not even sure this contract makes sense. Enjoy.

This "scared-straight" contract goes into effect on _____, the ____ day of the month of _____, in the year _____, and remains in effect for one calendar year upon signing. Because of the seriousness of the ramifications herein, there is very rarely, if ever, cause for renewal.

I HAVE READ THIS AGREEMENT, I HAVE TAKEN TIME TO CONSIDER ITS IMPLICATIONS, I KIND OF DON'T MIND THIS AND WOULD SE-CRETLY BUY THE SALAD DRESSING AT THE GROCERY STORE, I FULLY UNDERSTAND ITS CONTENTS, I AGREE TO ITS TERMS, AND I VOLUNTARILY SUBMIT TO ITS EXECUTION.

_____

Partner 1

_____

Partner 2

7.3 The Wow, Your Cooking Tastes Just Like Gordon Ramsey's Contract

If you encourage your partner to make something homemade, then you better pretend to like it, or else they'll never cook for you again! And they will also resent you forever. Just keep the hot sauce and salt close by for frantic dousings when they turn their back.

_____ (Partner 1) and _____ (Partner 2), hereinafter referred to as "the Couple," agree not to trash each other's cooking. The Couple is also encouraged to say things like, "Mmmm . . . this is really yummy," "I really like the flavor," "This is awesome! It is a treat for my mouth!" _____, and _____ (positive comments about partner's cooking). Insulting a dish your partner slaved over can have dire repercussions (of which the male author of this book knows all too well, as he once spit out a piece of key lime pie the female author of this book made and further insulted her by using the term "gag reflex" when he attempted to apologize).

If said partner does not have the best of cooking skills (and that's putting it nicely), the other partner needs to "man up" and just eat the damn thing and then just pretend they have IBS and need to run to the bathroom, where they can regurgitate it if necessary. Sorry, this just got really gross. Or just say "Thank you" and swallow it, OK? There are worse tragedies in the world.

The Couple agrees they will encourage each other to experiment in the kitchen (not just sexually), trying to make things such as _____, _____ , and _____. And even when it all goes terribly wrong, the Couple agrees to be chill and nice about it.

I HAVE READ THIS AGREEMENT, I HAVE TAKEN TIME TO CONSIDER ITS IMPLICATIONS, I WILL NOT BE A BITCH ABOUT LOUSY

HOMEMADE FOOD, I AGREE TO ITS TERMS, AND I VOLUNTARILY SUBMIT TO ITS FLAVORLESS EXECUTION.

_____

Partner 1

_____

Partner 2

7.4 The Let's Make Believe It's 1957 and Sit at the Fucking Table Contract

Eye contact and actually listening to another human being speak—I know it sounds weird, but in moderation it can be good for you. Actually eat at the table (not in front of a myriad of screens while lazing on the couch) and act as if being civilized still matters and is respected (what a farce, but we wish it did). Force yourselves to make relatively normal, semi-meaningful conversation, asking each other stuff like, "How was your day, dear?" "How's that rash coming along?"—you know, crap like that.

_____ (Partner 1) and _____ (Partner 2), hereinafter referred to as "the Couple," agree to eat dinner together _____ nights per week on _____ (list day(s) of the week), seated at an arranged grouping of furniture items known as "the Table." "Dinner" is to be defined as a home-cooked meal (or, for lazy people, takeout that you must put on real plates). Extra points: Why not even prepare the meal together?! (This is getting out of hand.) The Couple agrees to each leave their respective phones in a different room, or at least not to have them out on the table or hidden in their laps under the Table (nice try).

To fill any awkward, deafening silences that they usually don't even notice because of the opiate of the masses (screens), the Couple may draw from the following rousing icebreakers (in addition to the afore-mentioned doozies):

"How was your afternoon (or morning)?"

"Did we get any mail today?"

"How did you sleep last night?"

"Any interesting dreams recently?"

"I think I might be getting a cold. You?"

"Do you think we will find life on any exoplanets anytime soon?"

"Remember that hilarious contracts book?"

_____

_____

_____

_____

The Let's Make Believe It's 1957 and Sit at the Table Contract will expire one calendar year after signing, honey!

I HAVE READ THIS AGREEMENT, I HAVE TAKEN TIME TO CONSIDER ITS IMPLICATIONS, THIS DOESN'T SEEM SO BAD, I AM ONLY MILDLY NERVOUS ABOUT MAKING POLITE SMALL TALK WITH MY PARTNER, I AGREE TO ITS TERMS, AND I VOLUNTARILY SUBMIT TO ITS EXECUTION.

_____
Partner 1

_____
Partner 2 ("2" may indicate inferior status in keeping with '50s theme)

7.5 The Grow Up and Eat Your Damn Vegetables Contract

Agree to eat a set amount of veggie servings every week while perhaps even limiting junk food intake (we know, that's crazy). If you have dueling Fun Dip and McDonald's addictions like the male coauthor of this book, buttress this contract with professional help and perhaps a couple support groups.

_____ (Partner 1) and _____ (Partner 2), hereinafter referred to as "the Couple," agree to eat _____ servings of vegetables per day/week/month (circle one) in a direct effort to eat more nutritious foodstuffs. A "serving" is defined as four ounces (about a half cup by volume, dingus) of a raw or cooked vegetable (no nitpicking here; tomatoes and green beans are friggin' vegetables). French fries do not count as a vegetable, and neither do tater tots (come on, guys), even (or especially) if they're hussied up with duck fat, truffle butter, etc. Sweet potato fries, in any form, will get you half credit (nice going).

In an effort to make this a successful, transparent co-effort, some vegetables that both Partners like and will readily eat together include _____, _____, _____, and _____ (list favorite or tolerated vegetables).

Moreover, the Couple agrees to limit their intake of fast food meals (this includes In-N-Out Burger, even though it could be successfully argued that In-N-Out makes you superhuman) to _____ meals per week/month/year (circle one, and no, we did not give you "day" as an option, chubs). Partner 1 and Partner 2 swear to God or the universe or the tree lords as their witness that they will not get fast food by themselves in secret because that is a shameful slippery slope.

I HAVE READ THIS AGREEMENT; I HAVE TAKEN TIME TO CONSIDER ITS IMPLICATIONS; I'M GOING TO STOP LIVING OFF PIZZA, COKE,

FRUIT GUSHERS, NILLA WAFERS, AND FRUITY PEBBLES; I AGREE TO ITS TERMS; AND I VOLUNTARILY SUBMIT TO ITS EXECUTION.

_____

Partner 1

_____

Partner 2

Part 8:
Entertainment and Outings

So where the hell have you guys been? "Super busy," huh? Things have been like "really crazy"? You guys have "a thing" to "take care of" and a "prescription and some ointment waiting at CVS," huh? Well, bitches, we are here to call bullshit. Face it; you guys have sunk deep into that love bubble, which is perfectly acceptable for a few months in the beginning of a relationship, right? I mean, who wants to be around a new couple or some lovesick dodo anyway? Barf. Well, if it's been a year, or seven, or twenty-five we think it's about time you guys got out a little. It'll be fun! Or at the very least, if one of you has been complaining about this, you will have to shut up for a while.

☐ 8.1 THE GO OUT AND DO FUN STUFF CONTRACT

☐ 8.2 THE SHIT NOBODY WANTS TO GO TO BUT IS FORCED
TO GO TO ANYWAY CONTRACT

☐ 8.3 THE NETFLIX AND CHILL (NOT KILL) CONTRACT

☐ 8.4 THE IT'S CALLED AN OFF BUTTON CONTRACT

☐ 8.5 THE IKEA KØNTRÅKT

☐ 8.6 THE LET'S GET OUR STORIES STRAIGHT BEFORE
THIS LAME-ASS DINNER PARTY STARTS CONTRACT

8.1 The Go Out and Do Fun Stuff Contract

Force each other to get off the couch and get some goddamn fresh air before the Earth runs out of it—maybe a night out, day/road trip, we don't fucking know. Figure it out. Just leave the damn house and do something, damn it! Don't worry, Netflix will still be waiting for you when you get back.

_____ (Partner 1) and _____ (Partner 2), hereinafter referred to as "the Couple," hereby declare they will henceforth get off their asses and do More Stuff on _____, the ____ day of the month of _____, in the year of Beelzebub (he's a real character) _____. "More Stuff" is defined as any activity that takes place outside the home (or yard . . . so yes, this excludes barbecues, gardening, getting the mail, and other fake outings for agoraphobes).

The Couple agrees to go out and do something together, or together with friends, at least _____ times a week/month/year (circle one). Examples include checking out the new 1930s Panama Canal clipper ship–themed tiki bar (we know, it's so far and will take so much effort for everyone to put on real going-outside pants and to walk/drive three blocks, but just do it), _____, _____, and _____. Or go on a hike and get some vitamin D because every idiot likes hiking, and you don't really have to look as nice or talk as much. The Couple acknowledges it is truly in everyone's best interest to occasionally see the light of day and even socialize with other adult humans, even if being out in public is literal torture and you are both aliens in people costumes.

I HAVE READ THIS AGREEMENT, I HAVE TAKEN AS MUCH TIME AS POSSIBLE TO CONSIDER ITS IMPLICATIONS, I FULLY UNDER-STAND ITS CONTENTS, I AGREE TO ITS TERMS, I WILL CRAWL OUT

OF MY HOLE, AND I VOLUNTARILY SUBMIT TO ITS EXECUTION, I
GUESS.

_____

Partner 1

_____

Partner 2

8.2 The Shit Nobody Wants to Go to but Is Forced to Go to Anyway Contract

Agree to attend a set amount of lame parties and events, such as your partner's nephew's baptism, your partner's brother's girlfriend's birthday, your partner's psychologically degrading work holiday party, and other BS you don't want to go to but will be forced to go to anyway.

_____ (Partner 1) and _____ (Partner 2), hereafter referred to as "the Couple," hereby declare they will endure, at most, _____ (numerical digit) events where one Partner, hereinafter referred to as "the Invited Partner," requires the attendance of the other, hereinafter referred to as "the Plus One," whether it's to make them look cooler or nicer than they actually are, to provide comfort and/or be used as a visual obstruction (aka human shield) in terrifying social situations, and so on.

Once the limit of _____ events has been successfully endured by the Plus One in the given time frame, they are henceforth exempt from attending any more lame-ass, excruciating events they don't want to go to, although they may continue to use such events as excuses not to have to do things with other people, if desired, and may even take pleasure in accepting sympathy and even praise for their stoicism: "Such a bummer, dude." "Much commitment, partner. Wow."

The Couple agrees to maintain a written tally of events attended, so they don't forget how many shitty events they've attended together and argue about it. Partners may draw frowny faces in the margins as desired.

The Couple makes this vow, hereafter referred to as, simply, I Will Bust You in the Kneecap with a Crowbar and Physically Drag You to This if I Have To, on _____, the ____ day of the month of _____, in the year _____. This contract expires one calendar year from the date of signing.

I HAVE READ THIS AGREEMENT, I HAVE TAKEN AS MUCH TIME AS POSSIBLE TO CONSIDER ITS IMPLICATIONS, I FULLY UNDER-STAND ITS CONTENTS, I AGREE TO ITS TERMS, I REALLY FUCKING HATE THIS, AND I VOLUNTARILY SUBMIT TO ITS EXECUTION.

_____
Partner 1

_____
Partner 2

8.3 The Netflix and Not Kill Contract

Agree on a complete Netflix series or movie to watch together. And we mean *together*! Watching ahead on one's own is cruel behavior, and pretending you haven't already seen an episode is stressful, takes a lot of energy, and pretty much never works. You should probably make photocopies of this one, as this is one of the toughest issues couples face today.

_____ (Partner 1) and _____ (Partner 2), hereinafter referred to as "the Couple," hereby declare they will exercise control over solo, obsessive, antisocial, masturbatory, psychotic individual binge-watching, inclusive of watching ahead of one's partner, hereinafter referred to as "the Netflix Self-Control Principle" on _____, the _____ day of the month of _____, in the year _____.

The Netflix Self-Control Principle prohibits watching ahead of the other party of the Couple without express written consent to do so. This consent applies to situations where one party is away on a business trip, in rehab (to treat acute binge-watching and/or masturbation addiction), in a mental hospital (for binge-watching and/or meth psychosis and/or masturbation addiction; especially in cases where the meth was used to keep the individual awake so they could continue to binge-watch and/or masturbate), physically incapacitated (especially from nerve deadening due to binge-watching and . . . well, you know); or simply asleep, doing "volunteer work," on a trip to the grocery store, _____, _____, or _____. If consent is given, this agreement stipulates the impatient, selfish, *Dance Moms*–addicted partner must not divulge any plot developments (i.e., Chloe wins nationals), character developments, deaths, births, affairs, etc. (hereafter referred to as the "Super-Important Events in Streaming

Content, and therefore Super Important in My Actual Life, Which Is Kind of Sad Clause").

Moreover, the Couple agrees to watch season _____ of the television or web series _____, hereinafter referred to as "the Show," together in its entirety. No episodes of the Show may be viewed by either partner without the other present. If one partner is asleep, that does not constitute "present." Both partners must be awake and facing the screen at time of viewing. Brisk but gentle slapping in the head/neck area, propping eyelids open, or _____ is acceptable.

The Netflix and Chill (Not Kill) Contract will expire upon viewing completion of the Show.

I HAVE READ THIS AGREEMENT, I HAVE TAKEN TIME TO CONSIDER ITS IMPLICATIONS, I FULLY UNDERSTAND ITS CONTENTS, I AGREE TO ITS TERMS, I VOLUNTARILY SUBMIT TO ITS EXECUTION, AND I READ THIS WHOLE DOCUMENT WITHOUT FALLING ASLEEP.

_____

Partner 1

_____

Partner 2

Note: if you're too cool for Netflix and use some other streaming content service, pirated or otherwise, this contract will also apply to that bullshit too.

8.4 The It's Called an Off Button Contract

Your eyes and motor skills are failing due to excessive screen time; you're drooling staring at a Reddit thread about K-Beauty. It's time to take a break, go for a walk (once your legs wake up in about an hour), read a book, or even take a nap (baby steps). Set daily or weekly screen-time limits and have weekly nonelectronic fun of some kind (yes, it's still possible).

_____ (Partner 1) and _____ (Partner 2), hereinafter referred to as "the Couple," hereby declare they will enact time restrictions on the usage of electronic devices (iPads, iPhones, laptops, Game Boys), hereinafter referred to as "Screen-Free Time," on _____, the ____ day of the month of _____, in the year of our iLord _____. The Couple agrees to go completely Screen-Free for _____ minutes/hours/days (circle one) of the day/week/fortnight/month (circle one).

During a vacation, defined as an out-of-town trip of three or more days, the Couple agrees only to use *their own* respective devices for _____ minutes/hours of each day. This clause may include DSLR cameras but not analog SLRs (because if you're using a real SLR, you are probably pretty cool and not annoyingly tech-obsessed).

Moreover, the Couple agrees to grant their phones a little R&R. During Screen-Free Time, the Couple is encouraged to occasionally shut them off and set them out of view in a closet or drawer, off the charger. Alternatively, you may tuck them into tiny doll beds you just happen to have. Trust that your phones will be just fine without you, and you without them. The hardest part is letting go, but in the end it will make you stronger. As for your phones, maybe it's good for the battery life? We aren't sure. We're not techies.

The It's Called an Off Button Contract will expire one year (yeah, it just got real) after the date of signing.

I HAVE READ THIS AGREEMENT, I HAVE TAKEN TIME TO CONSIDER ITS IMPLICATIONS, I FULLY UNDERSTAND ITS CONTENTS, I AGREE TO ITS TERMS, I DON'T KNOW WHO I AM WITHOUT MY PHONE, I AM GOING TO MISS MY PHONE DEARLY, IT IS MY ONLY REAL FRIEND, I LOVE MY PHONE SO MUCH, OH GOD, MY PHONE . . . AND I VOLUNTARILY SUBMIT TO ITS EXECUTION.

_____
Partner 1

_____
Partner 2

8.5 The IKEA Køntråkt

Congrats on moving in together / buying a house / having a baby! You know what that means . . . time to go to IKEA! If the two of you can visit IKEA and complete a full, demented loop through the store without breaking up, having a nervous breakdown, going to prison for aggravated (and we mean *aggravated*) assault, hanging yourself by the cord of the VITEMÖLLA lamp, or smashing (or using) a display toilet, congrats. If not, it's OK and quite normal, and this contract is for you.

_____ (Partner 1) and _____ (Partner 2), hereinafter referred to as "the Couple," state heretofore, in the eyes of the law and all those cheap, demented freaks who shop and work at IKEA, that when they go to IKEA, if that is their wont, they will get through the experience without having total meltdowns or lashing out at each other, strangers, or staff, and will exit the "store" (see *maze of hell*) with only the items they came for, and maybe just a few FADO and MÖLLARP for the kitchen thrown in, as well as _____, _____, and _____ for the _____, and a belly full of two-dollar meatballs.

To reiterate, refrain from killing each other, perspiring to death from the anxiety and confusion of the "store," and buying a bunch of crap you don't need (besides MÖLLARP). Just pretend you're not a sentient human and follow the arrows, OK? If you start thinking too much—about how absurd the situation is, how claustrophobic it is, how hot it is, where or how any emergency exits could possibly even exist—your sense of time and space will warp and the real world will become a distant and rapidly fading memory, and that's when the mental chaos will begin, which could result in a pile of bodies stacked on the BRIMNES beds.

This life- and sanity-saving contract will expire on _____, after which we pray that the Couple will not need to revisit IKEA for another ten years, at minimum. If you must return sooner, just make a copy of this contract, cross out the dates (and partner, if you're in a new relationship, you TROLLØP), and save yet more "innocent" lives. Nothing against the people running IKEA or the freak Swede who founded it and is hiding his gargantuan wealth in a shell foundation, but this place is pretty whack. That said, you can get a great deal on a quality stain-resistant BEDDINGE LÖVÅS, which the entire family can sleep on.

I HAVE READ THIS AGREEMENT, I HAVE TAKEN TIME TO CONSIDER ITS IMPLICATIONS, I FULLY UNDERSTAND ITS CONTENTS, I AM PRETTY SURE I AM NOT A ZOMBIE SPAWNED BY THE FOUNDER OF IKEA (WITH A 90 PERCENT CONFIDENCE INTERVAL), I AGREE TO ITS TERMS, AND I VOLUNTARILY SUBMIT TO ITS EXECUTION.

_____
Partner 1

_____
Partner 2

8.6 The Let's Get Our Stories Straight Before This Lame-Ass Dinner Party Starts Contract

OK, so if you're reading this book, there's a good chance you met online—and we mean that as a compliment. It means you have a good sense of humor. But now you have to figure out how to lie about it . . . because it still is kind of embarrassing. Agree on a realistic "how we met" story and vow not to reveal embarrassing details about your partner such as their penchant for drinking in the middle of the workday and their obsession with white-noise machines.

_____ (Partner 1) and _____ (Partner 2), hereinafter referred to as "the Couple," agree to uphold a fabricated story about how they met, hereinafter referred to as "the Huge Lie Our Relationship Is Sort of Centered Around," on _____, the ____ day of the month of _____, in the year of our Liar _____.

The Huge Lie Our Relationship Is Sort of Centered Around is to take the place of the truth, which may be too embarrassing, depressingly boring, or annoying/difficult to explain to certain friends and family (for example, having met on Tinder or OkCupid, in an AOL *Buffy the Vampire Slayer* chat room, at the Olive Garden, on a drug run, at an orgy, at the Gap shopping for cords, at a Rob Lowe book signing, etc.).

The Huge Lie Our Relationship Is Sort of Centered Around is defined as follows: _____

_____

_____

_____.

Furthermore, Partner 1 agrees to hold the following shameful secrets about Partner 2 in the highest level of confidentiality and will do everything in his or her power to hide or cover up the following: ____

_____

_____

_____

_____ (i.e., they were in a sorority, they have a secret love child, they can't ride a bike, they own every Avril Lavigne album, or they can't really spell anything or read a map).

Furthermore, Partner 2 agrees to hold the following shameful secrets about Partner 1 in the highest level of confidentiality and will do everything in his or her power to hide or cover up the following: _____

_____

_____

_____

_____

_____.

The Let's Get Our Stories Straight before This Annoying Dinner Party Starts Contract exists in perpetuity, or until the disbandment of the Couple (circle one).

I HAVE READ THIS AGREEMENT, I HAVE TAKEN TIME TO CONSIDER ITS IMPLICATIONS, I FULLY UNDERSTAND ITS CONTENTS, I AGREE TO ITS TERMS, I AM PREPARED TO ROUTINELY LIE TO PEOPLE WHO "MATTER" TO ME, AND I VOLUNTARILY SUBMIT TO ITS EXECUTION.

_____
Partner 1

_____
Partner 2

PART 9:
Family and In-Laws

Naturally we all love/tolerate/fear our in-laws, or the family of our partner (if not married, just get married already. It's so great! . . . *Can she hear me? . . . Is she watching me? Where is she? Am I safe?* . . . See? Fun!). If you don't despise your in-laws (at least a little), there's definitely something wrong with you, you self-righteous a-hole. Normal human beings loathe their in-laws because they loathe us—among other reasons. But also because they get in your business and stay over at your house and complain about your towels and your coffee situation. Just kidding, there are cool in-laws out there . . . right? Hello? Anyone . . . ? To maintain harmony in the household of a (semi-?) committed couple, it's necessary for each partner to be nice to the other's horribly annoying, offensive, too fat / too thin, whiny, agonizingly boring family members. Just grit your teeth and pretend. You can do it!

☐ 9.1 THE BUT WE JUST SAW THEM CONTRACT

☐ 9.2 THE DON'T KILL OR BE KILLED BY YOUR PARTNER'S
     FAMILY CONTRACT

☐ 9.3 THE I HEAR IT'S SUPPOSED TO MAYBE RAIN ON
     THURSDAY . . . 60 PERCENT CHANCE THEY'RE SAYING
     NOW CONTRACT

☐ 9.4 THE AGREE TO SIDE WITH YOUR PARTNER IN THE
     PRESENCE OF IN-LAWS EVEN IF THEY HAVE THEIR FACTS
     WRONG AND YOU DON'T ACTUALLY AGREE WITH
     THEM CONTRACT

☐ 9.5 THE WHOSE PARENTS ARE WE VISITING THIS HOLIDAY?
     CONTRACT

9.1 The But We Just Saw Them Contract

Restrict the number of visits and lengths of visits to and from your intrusive, possessive, stunningly weird in-laws. It's for the best, and you deserve the best.

_____ (Partner 1) and _____ (Partner 2), hereinafter referred to as "the Couple," agree not to be complete psychopaths and to limit the number of visits to each other's parents'/family's homes.

Partner 1 hereby declares they will only drag Partner 2 to see their family or invite them to their own home (that's insane, considering all the porn and bizarre notes-to-self you keep around) _____ times a year, at maximum, and for only _____ days, and if they really care and want to do something nice for their partner, probably zero times, hereinafter referred to as the "Zero Rule." Hey, why not actually do something nice for your partner?

Further, Partner 2 hereby declares they will only drag Partner 1 to see their family or invite them to their own home _____ times a year, at maximum, and for only _____ days. Agree to keep the suffering short and sweet. Set the bar low, and watch your partner leap it with ease. Again, the Zero Rule also applies here. Sure, visiting family is nice in theory, and those bonds are eternal and whatever. But not seeing family at all is also a beautiful gesture. Absence makes the heart grow fonder, right? That's one of our favorite excuses for not doing stuff.

This high-stakes, critically important relationship maker-or-breaker contract will expire on _____, after which the Couple can reassess what worked and what didn't (if they're still together) and then make adjustments and reuse this contract accordingly.

I HAVE READ THIS AGREEMENT, I HAVE TAKEN TIME TO CONSIDER ITS IMPLICATIONS, I AGREE NOT TO SCREAM, "WHEN WILL THIS END?!" UNLESS EXTRAORDINARILY INTOXICATED AND INCOHERENT, I AGREE TO ITS TERMS, AND I VOLUNTARILY SUBMIT TO ITS EXECUTION.

_____

Partner 1

_____

Partner 2

9.2 The Don't Kill or Be Killed by Your Partner's Family Contract

There is no way of getting around it—you need to see the other half's family once in a while. This contract serves as assurance that your partner will be nice—or at least civil—to those assholes. Just for a few days. Lay out reasonable rules and etiquette for your in-laws while they're staying in your home, and make sure they've actually left before you go on an epic worthy-of-going-viral-on-YouTube, profanity-laced, hour-by-hour recap of their visit.

_____ (Partner 1) and _____ (Partner 2), hereinafter referred to as "the Couple" (or whatever the hell you want to be referred to), hereby declare they will make every effort, even in the face of egregious rudeness and complete lack of civility on their in-laws' part (this behavior should be expected, anticipated, even planned for) to be accommodating and pleasant (i.e., a fabulous opportunity to practice ironic and/or maniacal smiles / stares / feigned-interest expressions for one's own amusement). The Couple will treat their respective families with great "kindness" (or at least a lack of blatant loathing) on holidays, during non-holiday visits, and even on group vacations (no way, guys).

The Couple makes this vow, heretofore referred to as "the Vow" or "Oh God, I Just Heard the Doorbell; My In-Laws Are Here . . . Where Do I Hide?" on _____, the ____ day of the month of _____, in the year of our Lord (and you'll need Him now more than ever) _____. The Vow prohibits any and all slap-boxing matches, food poisonings, _____, _____ (ouch), _____ (that's sick!), excessively vitriolic verbal tirades, evil eyes (well, you can have one or two of those), and murder attempts during in-law visits.

Exceptions, with written consent from your partner, can be agreed upon as you wish (list here:_____, _____, _____). Examples of exceptions include a given in-law provoking a member of the Couple with comments about their weight, grooming habits, lack of intelligence, lousy cooking, poor housekeeping, or general unworthiness to be with their child . . . or alive.

I HAVE READ THIS AGREEMENT, I HAVE TAKEN TIME TO CONSIDER ITS IMPLICATIONS, I FULLY UNDERSTAND ITS CONTENTS, I AGREE TO ITS TERMS, I WILL BE NICE, I WILL BE NICE, I WILL BE NICE, AND I VOLUNTARILY SUBMIT TO ITS EXECUTION.

_____
Partner 1

_____
Partner 2

9.3 The I Hear It's Supposed to Maybe Rain on Thursday . . . 60 Percent Chance They're Saying Now Contract

When it comes to chatting with in-laws, most topics can be controversial. Agree that any discussions about politics, religion, sex, physical appearance / weight gain are absolutely off limits and should be instantly diverted to banter about the weather or benign personal health issues such as light rain / drizzle, wind gust speed and direction, pollen level alerts, how hot summer can be sometimes, nagging toe injuries, and ointments, rashes, hangnails, etc.

_____ (Partner 1) and _____ (Partner 2), hereinafter referred to as "the Couple," hereby declare when interacting with their in-laws they will make every effort to steer conversations to the most mundane, meaningless, shoot-me-in-the-face-boring topics, such as the weather, the foliage (or lack thereof), produce (although be careful, this can get testy, especially when it comes to apples), driving times from various locations to other locations, _____, _____, _____, and traffic patterns in various cities.

In a good-faith attempt to maintain good family relations, the Couple vows that if at any point a conversation veers remotely toward explosive hot topics such as politics (and specifically immigration), the NFL, brocialism, Islam, protestors, Kanye, Red Vines vs. Twizzlers, your "future," your reproductive plans, your stuff in their attic, _____, _____, _____, or _____, they will immediately and cheerfully (if possible) derail the conversation with a softball non sequitur.

In the event of a code-red conversation emergency, you may redirect to one of these hopefully safe topics (but we can't really promise you anything):

"How did you sleep last night?"

"Would you like some grapes?"

"Any upcoming travel plans?"

"Some weather, eh?"

"It's weird, I used to like salted saltines and now I prefer unsalted. Weird, right? You?"

_____

_____

_____

The Couple makes this vow, hereafter referred to as "Did You Hear That Ritz Crackers Are Going Back to Their Original Packaging?" on _____, the ____ day of the month of _____, in the year ____.

I HAVE READ THIS AGREEMENT, I HAVE TAKEN TIME TO CONSIDER ITS IMPLICATIONS, I FULLY UNDERSTAND ITS CONTENTS, I AGREE TO ITS TERMS, AGAIN, MY IN-LAWS SUCK AND ALL THEIR VIEWS ARE WHACK-ASS, BUT THAT'S OK, AND I VOLUNTARILY SUBMIT TO ITS EXECUTION.

_____
Partner 1

_____
Partner 2

9.4 The Agree to Side with Your Partner in the Presence of In-laws Even if They Have Their Facts Wrong and You Don't Actually Agree with Them Contract

After a while, or even right away, things can get dicey when it comes to family. Don't upset your partner by siding with your own blood relatives too often, since they will likely be busy sniffing out your sweetheart's weak spots and looking to start a competition of some kind. It's probably instinctual, which it's not to say it's not awful. Instincts can be awful. Fill this one out and see if it eases any tension. God bless.

_____ (Partner 1) and _____ (Partner 2), hereinafter referred to as "the Couple," hereby declare they will always and without question side with their partner when conflicts or even the most minuscule tensions arise (because they never _really are_ minuscule) between their partner and their parent(s), especially in the realms of food storage and preparation, work-life balance, liking or disliking a particular celebrity, historical facts, fashion trends, _____, _____, and _____. Simply put, each Partner agrees always to side with their partner over their parents, whom they probably resent anyway for some juvenile reason.

The Couple acknowledges that all forms of opinions, unsolicited advice, generosity, _____, _____, _____, and criticism from in-laws are maneuvers in a masterfully evil mind-fuck game of allegiance, i.e., if you start buying the paper towels your mom insists are better than the inferior ones your (implied inferior) partner usually buys, well, you're feeding the goddamn beast. Buy the shitty paper towels, damn it!

The easiest, most natural approach is to feign ignorance or impartiality when your partner is feuding with your parents, but the Couple agrees that this hangs your partner out to dry and your parents will undoubt-edly tout it as a victory. Each Partner agrees to stop this kind of loyalty showdown madness by swooping in and affirming their partner's view with gusto by stating something like, "Yeah, Natalie Portman *does* seem pretty annoying" or, "Yeah, the Constitution *was* written in 1776" (it was not). Great job, Partner!

The Couple makes this vow of primary loyalty, referred to as "You Are My #1 Top Dog, and My Parents Are Lower-Ranking Dogs" on _____, the ____ day of the month of _____, in the year _____.

I HAVE READ THIS AGREEMENT, I HAVE TAKEN TIME TO CONSIDER ITS IMPLICATIONS, I FULLY UNDERSTAND ITS CONTENTS, I AGREE TO ITS TERMS, I WILL ALWAYS DUTIFULLY DEFEND AND AGREE WITH MY PARTNER NO MATTER HOW DUMB, GROSS, OR WEIRD THEY ARE / ARE BEING, AND I VOLUNTARILY SUBMIT TO ITS EX-ECUTION.

_____
Partner 1

_____
Partner 2

9.5 The Whose Parents Are We Visiting This Holiday? Contract

Where did we go last? The Cleve or the 'Dacks (Adirondacks, to visit your shut-in upstate New York hillbilly relatives for Christmas)? Who can remember, as we've blocked out most of those holiday family trips due to emotional trauma and epic life-sucking boredom.

_____ (Partner 1) and _____ (Partner 2), hereinafter referred to as "the Couple," agree to schedule regular holiday visits that repeat year after year in a sad, predictable hell-spiral until you or everyone you know has mercifully died off, hereafter referred to as "The Holiday Visit Pact."

Having dug deep into the darkest corners of their repressed collective subconscious, the Couple can verifiably state that the most recent _____ (list holiday) was spent with the family of Partner 1 / 2 (circle one), the most recent _____ (list holiday) was spent with the family of Partner 1 / 2 (circle one), and bless your poor souls if you require a third mandatory holiday visit, the most recent _____ (list holiday) was spent with the family of Partner 1 / 2 (circle one). The Couple agrees to hereafter alternate destinations each year (or family invited if choosing to host family; shudder), based on these most recent instances beginning on _____, the ____ day of the month of _____, in the year of Beelzebub (lucky you if your family members are Satan worshipers; sounds like that could at least bring with it some interesting holiday games/cuisine/sauces).

The Couple may diverge from the schedule if one or more Partners is injured or falls ill (no faking; see the That Cough Sounds Fake Contract) and the Couple is unable to travel, or if special titillating circumstances arise, for example, if Partner 2's family invites you to an all-expenses-paid chateau rental in the South of France, even though you spent

Christmas with those dickbags last year. After which, the alternating schedule would resume as normal. We don't really know anyone who gets to do that kind of stuff, but if you find this clause useful, good on you and God bless! Marry that spoiled brat already!

Going forward, the Couple will make sure to write down where they go on a given holiday, put it in their blackberries or pagers, or remember to beep each other if they're those high-tech types, and then cross-reference with this contract to be sure they're properly alternating and spreading all the anxiety and dread out evenly. That's what couple-dom is about, after all! Compromise. Making the other partner happy. And hot/tepid sex in your childhood bedroom.

I HAVE READ THIS AGREEMENT, I HAVE TAKEN TIME TO CONSIDER ITS IMPLICATIONS, I AGREE TO ITS TERMS, I WILL NOT FAKE ANY INJURIES, PREGNANCIES, OR MY OWN DEATH TO GET OUT OF VISITING MY PARTNER'S FAMILY, AND I VOLUNTARILY SUBMIT TO ITS EXECUTION.

_____

Partner 1

_____

Partner 2

PART 10:

Chores and Other 'Round-the-House BS

Chores suck! Especially if your parents were half-assed about making you do them as a kid. Who knew that you can spend an entire weekend just doing basic chores? If one or more of you weirdos actually enjoys folding laundry or doing dishes, good for you. Congrats! As if chores and household crap don't suck enough, other people can be super-specific assholes about how to—say, for instance—fold a hand towel. Have no fear, you'll be whistling and working together in harmony and birds will be tying your apron strings once you fill out these contracts.

☐ 10.1 THE WE'RE SUCH FUCKING SLOBS CONTRACT

☐ 10.2 THE FURNITURE ASSEMBLY AND DISASSEMBLY
         DUTIES AND BEHAVIORS CONTRACT

☐ 10.3 THE YOU'RE BECOMING A SHUT-IN HOARDER
         CONTRACT

☐ 10.4 THE I'M NOT YOUR MOTHER CONTRACT

10.1 The We're Such Fucking Slobs Contract

Assign horrible but very necessary chores and cleaning tasks, such as taking out the ten-day-old trash, trying and failing to fold pizza boxes, locating stray Hot Pockets inside furniture, etc. Sign this binding contract, and there will be no confusion about which one of you needs to stop throwing clothes all over the house like an angsty fourteen-year-old.

_____ (Partner 1) and _____ (Partner 2), hereinafter referred to as "the Couple," agree to take regular actions to coexist in a relatively tidy space, like grown-ups, hereinafter referred to as the "Let's Not Live in a Dumpster Contract" on _____, the ____ day of the month of _____, in the year _____.

This agreement enlists each Partner to take action to routinely refrain from their most egregious and disgusting displays of slobbery, hereinafter referred to as "Filth Bombs."

Partner 1 will devote regular time to the management of the following Filth Bombs: _____

_____

_____

_____ (i.e., loose balls of hairbrush hair; hair everywhere except in the trash; wayward stiff, sweaty socks; dirty dishes "soaking" in limbo and shame; used dental floss draped about lighting fixtures and faucets; tortured mounds of junk mail waiting to be put out of its misery; toenail clippings left near to where people eat; etc.).

Partner 2 will devote regular time to the management of the following Filth Bombs: _____

_____

_____

_____ (Ew ew ew ew ew ew ew ew ew ew. Ew. Gross.)

The Let's Not Live in a Dumpster contract expires on _____, or when the couple disbands.

I HAVE READ THIS AGREEMENT, I HAVE TAKEN TIME TO CONSIDER ITS IMPLICATIONS, I FULLY UNDERSTAND ITS CONTENTS, I WILL BE LESS GROSS, I AGREE TO ITS TERMS, AND I VOLUNTARILY SUBMIT TO ITS EXECUTION.

_____

Partner 1

_____

Partner 2

10.2 The Furniture Assembly and Disassembly Duties and Behaviors Contract

"Do these instructions only come in Mandarin?! Because that's all I'm seeing here! Fuuuuuuucccccckkkkk!" Figure out who is less of a spaz when it comes to furniture assembly, and assign duties, and enact and enforce accordingly.

_____ (Partner 1) and _____ (Partner 2), hereinafter referred to as "the Couple," hereby declare they will bar the partner with zero (or accepted inferior) mechanical inclination, also known as the "Couldn't Assemble a Decent-Looking Mr. Potato Head Partner," herein referred to as the Potato Head Partner, from attempting to assemble, co-assemble (with the Mechanically Inclined Partner), or backseat assemble any products or pieces of furniture requiring any degree of assemblage, hereinafter referred to as "The Great Assembly Ban," on _____, the _____ day of the month of _____, in the year _____.

The Great Assembly Ban explicitly prohibits the Potato Head Partner from weighing in, in any capacity, or even directly observing the work of the Mechanically Inclined Partner in action. The former may not offer to get the latter so much as a glass of water or a flashlight or offer any assistance under what are clearly false pretenses.

If the Mechanically Inclined Partner requires help, usually in the form of simple brut force or stabilization, they may enlist the Potato Head Partner, who must take orders and perform the requested task(s) in bone-chilling silence, like a robot. The Mechanically Inclined Partner must then dismiss the Potato Head Partner with the following non-verbal cue: _____. The Potato Head Partner, who may coincidentally be the chattier partner, acknowledges that silence is of critical importance in these circumstances. The intense, Mechanically

117

Inclined Partner will likely be cursing to themselves, and a simple, "Hey wha—" can easily and justly warrant a "Fuck off!" or a stray slat thrown in response. Furthermore, the Potato Head Partner agrees never, *ever* to look at the directions, ask to look at the directions, touch the directions, smell the directions, speak of the directions, badmouth the directions, think of the directions, or gesture in the direction of the directions.

The Great Assembly Ban will expire on _____, thus totaling ____ days/weeks/months (circle one) in duration.

I HAVE READ THIS AGREEMENT, I HAVE TAKEN TIME TO CON-SIDER ITS IMPLICATIONS, I FULLY UNDERSTAND ITS CONTENTS, I SOLEMNLY SWEAR NOT TO STAB MY PARTNER WITH AN ALLEN WRENCH, I AGREE TO ITS TERMS, AND I VOLUNTARILY SUBMIT TO ITS EXECUTION.

_____

Partner 1 (Mechanically Inclined)

_____

Partner 2 (Potato Head)

10.3 The You're Becoming a Shut-In Hoarder Contract

We know this is an age of prosperity in the Western world, but stop buying crap you don't need, dudes! At least dial it down. Agree upon anti-hoarding routines for purging material possessions, and have a yard sale to get rid of all your useless crap—like your eleventh and twelfth white-noise machines, and the dysfunctional ones that sound as if there are satanic messages hidden amidst the fuzz. (What's with our obsession with white-noise machines?)

_____ (Partner 1) and _____ (Partner 2), hereinafter referred to as "the Couple," hereby declare they will limit the number of belongings they own, individually or together, and take actions to regularly get rid of stuff so they don't end up like the Collyer brothers or a crazy person on TV, hereinafter referred to as "the Hoarder Contract," on _____, the ____ day of the month of _____, in the year of the _____ (enter Norse god of your choice) _____ (year).

The shopaholic and/or hoarding, newspaper-collecting type could be Partner 1, Partner 2, or both (circle), hereafter referred to as the "Crap Magnet(s)." Because decluttering is a spiritual art form, we present you with the following options (choose as many as are needed):

For every _____ nominal acquisition(s) (i.e., Amazon banana slicers, free promotional tchotchkes, bottles of hotel shampoo, _____, _____), then _____ items must be thrown out or placed in a bag to donate, which must be done within ___ days from the start date of _____, along with any other crap you amass along the way.

Pick up a copy of Marie Kondo's _The Life-Changing Magic of Tidying Up_, maybe smoke some weed, and think about how your belongings might feel stressed out, cramped, and neglected because, perhaps, *you are the real garbage?* The Crap Magnet(s) agrees to do everything Marie says.

For the next _____ week(s)/month(s)/day(s)/year(s) (circle one), throw away or donate (see previous page re: donation guidelines, you lazy bastards) _____ item(s) every minute/hour/day/month (circle one).

The Crap Magnet(s) will organize and execute a yard / tag / garage / rummage / stoop / whatever the hell you call it sale _____ time(s) every fiscal quarter/year (circle one).

The Hoarder Contract will expire on _____, thus totaling _____ days/weeks/months/years (circle one) in duration.

I HAVE READ THIS AGREEMENT, I HAVE TAKEN TIME TO CONSIDER ITS IMPLICATIONS, I FULLY UNDERSTAND ITS CONTENTS, I AGREE TO ITS TERMS, I VOLUNTARILY SUBMIT TO ITS EXECUTION, AND I WILL NOT IMMEDIATELY LOSE THIS PAPER IN THE SWIRLING TRASH HOLE THAT IS OUR SHARED LIVING SPACE.

_____
Partner 1

_____
Partner 2

10.4 The I'm Not Your Mother Contract

Establish that neither partner has been enlisted as a stand-in for their weird mom, and neither partner should expect the other to pick up after them, do *alllll* the laundry, spontaneously/desperately present them with snack foods, or pack them lunches with creepy notes inside.

_____ (Partner 1) and _____ (Partner 2), hereinafter referred to as "the Couple," hereby declare neither Partner will expect the other Partner to act as a substitute mom*, hereinafter referred to as the "I'm Not Your Goddamn Weird Mom, Asshole! Contract," on _____, the ____ day of the month of _____, in the year _____.

The Couple acknowledges and accepts that when a couple lives together and attains a level of comfort with one another, Partners reveal the sickest, most depraved features of their truest selves. (Hobbes was right—if you don't understand that basic reference, please go read a fucking book—this one definitely doesn't count.) One such feature being that they're a completely helpless mama's boy (or girl) who would easily die if left alone for a few days due to a complete lack of basic self-reliance skills.

Each Partner understands they are never to expect the other to pander to their every need like a servant, literally run around and pick up after them like a cartoon, lavish them in a stream of completely unfounded compliments, wash and fold and put away all their clothes all the time, surprise them with Sunny D and Totino's Pizza Rolls, congratulate them for finishing their dinner, _____, _____, and _____. You can still get your Partner to do stuff for you, but do offer something in exchange, or at least frickin' ask politely—or you will plant deep seeds of resentment that will grow and blossom into outbursts of raaaaaage!

Upon signing the I'm Not Your Goddamn Weird Mom, Asshole! Contract, it exists in perpetuity, so get it together, people.

I HAVE READ THIS AGREEMENT, I HAVE TAKEN TIME TO CONSIDER ITS IMPLICATIONS, I FULLY UNDERSTAND ITS CONTENTS, I AGREE TO ITS TERMS, I DO KNOW HOW TO DO MY OWN LAUNDRY AND WOULD *NEVER PRETEND NOT TO*, AND I VOLUNTARILY SUBMIT TO ITS EXECUTION.

_____
Partner 1

_____
Partner 2

*Daddy issues are also discouraged. We don't have time for that contract now, though, sickies.

PART 11:

"Us," or Miscellaneous Couples Crap

You are a unit, you two. You love each other, right? If not, don't answer that. Just look down at your phone and start swiping away like
a jag-off. Maybe your love is growing, maybe it is stagnant, maybe it
is floundering and you have turned to this book to save your relationship. While that is the most insane thing we have ever heard, we
appreciate the effort and the sale. Cha-ching! No matter how long
you've been a couple, there may be issues with important things like
trust and/or simply driving each other out of your minds. Whether
annoying little behaviors or disturbing big behaviors, these contracts
will address them and liquidate them, like the Terminator or Rambo
on steroids, if they are executed properly and with dedication. Even
behaviors like Jimmy legs or "rubby feet" can be stopped, and these
contracts will help you get there.

☐ 11.1 THE THEY'RE WATCHING, EVERYONE IS WATCHING,
      I'M NOT CRAZY, YOU'RE CRAZY, WHY IS IT SO HOT
      IN HERE? CONTRACT

☐ 11.2 THE CAN YOU GET OUT OF MY FACE FOR
      A GODDAMN SECOND SO I CAN BREATHE? CONTRACT

☐ 11.3 THE ARE THESE YOUR PANTIES OR MINE? CONTRACT

☐ 11.4 THE JUST SIT IN THE PASSENGER SEAT AND
      SHUT YOUR MOUTH! CONTRACT

☐ 11.5 THE ANNOYING PET PEEVES CONTRACT

☐ 11.6 THE WELCOME TO THE DOGHOUSE CONTRACT

11.1 The They're Watching, Everyone Is Watching, I'm Not Crazy, You're Crazy, Why Is It So Hot in Here? Contract

Agree to respect each other's privacy, including no snooping, no looking at your partner's Internet search history ("Why were you looking at freaky man-sized bunny pictures and how to escape to Mexico via DIY tunnels? Are those two things related?"), no phone monitoring, etc.

_____ (Partner 1) and _____ (Partner 2), hereinafter referred to as "the Couple," agree to respect one another's private space to a reasonable extent, trusting one another to conduct themselves as responsible adults in a committed relationship. Ahh, technology has afforded us many great things, hasn't it? Like emojis and the ability to lie about our psychological state to an array of "friends." But it has also provided opportunities to snoop and expose our Partner as the creep they may or may not be deep down in the bowels of their soul (yes, souls have bowels; we checked with a scientist).

Partner 1 hereby declares she/he will not snoop through Partner 2's phone, computer, journal, _____, _____, or any other device that may or may not hoard embarrassing information, notes to self, links to fringe self-help groups, or emails to/from WikiLeaks (we can all dream). Partner 2 makes the same vow to Partner 1, with the same level of rigidity. This contract takes precedence in normal, boring, wonderful, joyous day-to-day life.

However, and this is a big _however_, if there is probable cause, defined as _____, strange calls or texts in the middle of the night, _____, _____, one partner rushing out to bizarre, half-baked photo shoots and having new, sexy, and/or grungy photog friends in the mix, or laugh-riot Skype sessions with the Taliban,

the suspicious partner, within the bounds of sane action, may
_____, _____, or _____. We're leaving those
up to the Couple because we don't know how creepy you are, and this
one seems weird. Partner 1 and Partner 2 will make their best efforts to
stay respectful of one another's privacy on the Interwebs—accepting
that our Partners search for weird stuff online, may occasionally visit
unsavory sites, and may have secret actualized online personas with
nominal fan bases that you know literally nothing about.

I HAVE READ THIS AGREEMENT, I HAVE TAKEN TIME TO CONSIDER
ITS IMPLICATIONS, WE ARE PROBABLY NOT PARANOID ENOUGH
TO BE COMMITTED INVOLUNTARILY TO A BEHAVIORAL HEALTH
INPATIENT FACILITY (OUTPATIENT, SURE), I AGREE TO ITS TERMS,
AND I VOLUNTARILY SUBMIT TO ITS EXECUTION.

_____

Partner 1

_____

Partner 2

11.2 The Can You Get Out of My Face for a Goddamn Second So I Can Breathe? Contract

Agree upon periods of "me time," such as giving each other personal space—and time to watch that show your partner refuses to watch with you. Or even read a book (let's not get carried away with all the book talk) or walk around the block a few times, creeping out the neighbors, or climb up on the roof, stare at nothing, and just shut the fuck up for two seconds, heaven forbid!

_____ (Partner 1) and _____ (Partner 2), hereinafter referred to as "the Couple," hereby declare they will butt out of each other's business every so often and take some time away from each other— even . . . especially . . . if they cohabitate—in order to maintain sanity and affection for one another. If you're one of those super-annoying couples that need to be around each other every minute, a) it will wear off if you stay together long enough, and b) fuck you, why did you buy this book? Just kidding, we'll take the sale and we wish you the best. Thank you so, so much . . . tell your friends! We enter into this contract on _____, the ____ day of the month of _____, in the year _____.

This agreement reinforces the foundation of any great (see _decent_) relationship—time away from each other. Partner 1 and Partner 2 hereby declare they will give each other a minimum of _____ minutes/hours/ days (circle one) to themselves per day/week (circle one), during which time neither partner will infringe on the other's private thoughts, wall-staring, "journaling," _____, _____, actions, solitary drinking, and nonactions, unless mutually agreed upon and/or a fire starts in your apartment and only one exit is available (although you could just let one partner exit down the fire escape while the other counts off a few beats to let them continue to have their space; but keep it safe, guys, trust your survival instincts). Penalties for not obeying this "me time" contract include _____, _____, spiked paddle spankings, _____, and/or _____.

Moreover, the Couple agrees not to judge what they may have and may not have done during their respective private time, which may include things such as _____, seashell art, bad paintings, weak journaling, dancing angrily in an abandoned warehouse, _____, pretending to write (an atrocious screenplay, book, poem, school paper, personal anti-technology manifesto, whatever), and _____. That's why it's called "me time"; you're allowed to get as weird *with yourself* as you want, if you can read between the lines. No judgment.

The "Me Time" agreement shall expire on _____.

I HAVE READ THIS AGREEMENT, I HAVE TAKEN TIME TO CONSIDER ITS IMPLICATIONS, I KNOW I AM AN INDIVIDUAL HUMAN BEING AND I SHOULD BE ABLE TO BE ALONE SOMETIMES, I AGREE TO ITS TERMS, AND I VOLUNTARILY SUBMIT TO ITS EXECUTION.

_____

Partner 1

_____

Partner 2

11.3 The Are These Your Panties or Mine? Contract

Ban any and all words and terms you hate (i.e., *panties, pussy, bucket list, yolo, swag, fiancée, cankles, literally, bae, bruh/brah/bro, juxtapose, bromance, foodie, crust, lovemaking, preggers, hubby, selfie, butt hurt*—we didn't even want to type that one—*moist,* etc.).

_____ (Partner 1) and _____ (Partner 2), hereinafter referred to as "Never, Ever Say That Word Again, You Bastard/Bitch," agree to refrain from uttering words and phrases their partner despises. These terms/words, which make your partner's skin crawl, spine alight with rage, and cause their mind to shift into homicidal ideation, shall be avoided at all costs. The penalties for emitting these banned utterances include such things as _____, tongue removal, a long lecture about having class, bitch slapping, _____, and _____.

The Couple acknowledges there will probably be some terms/words one Partner can abide that the other partner cannot. For instance, *moist* seems to roil females more so than males, but this is not written in stone, of course. Be nice and don't hurt your Partner's ears with these vile words, even if they don't at all offend you. And in general the previous examples, and probably most of the words you come up with, are reprehensible and indefensible to pretty much everyone. The Couple agrees the following words shall nary again be spoken: _____, _____, _____, _____, _____, _____, _____, and _____.

(Note: Feel free to write additional words in the margins, as necessary, because we know language can be revolting . . . and beautiful.)

I HAVE READ THIS AGREEMENT, I HAVE TAKEN TIME TO CONSIDER ITS IMPLICATIONS, I AGREE TO THINK BEFORE I SPEAK AND NOT

TO CHOOSE DISGUSTING WORDS THAT MAKE ME SEEM LIKE A
HUMAN DUMPSTER, I AGREE TO ITS TERMS, AND I VOLUNTARILY
SUBMIT TO ITS EXECUTION.

_____
Partner 1

_____
Partner 2

11.4 The Just Sit in the Passenger Seat and Shut Your Mouth! Contract

Attention, backseat drivers . . . passenger-seat drivers . . . middle-seat bitch drivers. Assholes, assholes, assholes, all. Use this contract to ensure the partner behind the wheel can concentrate on the road and the rockin' tunes and not their fantasies about smacking their loudmouth, wrong-about-everything partner in their fat, rude face.

_____ (Partner 1) and _____ (Partner 2), hereinafter referred to as "the Couple," agree to refrain from piping up about their partner's driving (i.e., "That's not a yield sign; it's a sign for a roadside farm stand, you moron"), save for truly dangerous situations and/or if your partner is truly a horrible driver, in which case, get them lessons or something, you cheap fucks. Or just drive yourself, dick! Each Partner agrees not to say things like: "Maybe you should move over now, just to get in position," "Watch your speed," "Hey, take it easy on the brake," or "Floor it!" (unless you're fleeing from the cops with pounds of weed in the trunk, then the last one is fine), _____, _____, _____, and _____. These are just a few choice phrases to avoid. But this contract shall apply to more than just the aforementioned obnoxious phrases. It applies to a general pattern of behavior and tone of voice that adds nothing and only serves to irritate the actual driver/Partner. Signing this contract bars the passenger Partner from being a bossy, self-aggrandizing, egomaniacal, condescending force in the automobile, on a motorcycle, on a boat, or out on the water skis. Any time one Partner is steering and the other isn't, get it? If you are Richard Branson and steer your own yacht or spaceship, this contract still applies. The passenger Partner agrees to sit there and shut the fuck up. Again, if you're about to drive off a cliff or crash into Mars, feel free to pipe up (the authors are irrationally worried about liability here; as if anyone will take this sacred text remotely seriously).

Studies have shown* that having a jagoff passenger shooting their mouth off can actually *cause* accidents. The passenger Partner hereby swears to sit down, shut up, and eat their trail mix while pumping out serene vibes. Or better yet, agrees to act as DJ and say lovingly complimentary things about their Partner's driving, such as "Nice turn," "Your speed is perfect right now," "You're always in the proper lane, aren't you?" "You could be a professional driver . . . and I'm not necessarily talking about Uber!" _____, _____, and _____ while setting a calm tone with sweet mid- to down-tempo jams like _____, _____, _____, and "Mexico" by James Taylor.

I HAVE READ THIS AGREEMENT, I HAVE TAKEN TIME TO CONSIDER ITS IMPLICATIONS, I AGREE TO BE A SUPPORTIVE AND PRODUC-TIVE TEAM PLAYER IN THE CAR, TO NOT SCREAM UNLESS WE ARE CAREENING INTO A TREE, AND TO SELECT THE PROPER TUNES FOR THE PROPER SITUATION (IF GIVEN PERMISSION TO DO SO), I AGREE TO ITS TERMS, AND I VOLUNTARILY SUBMIT TO ITS EXECUTION.

_____

Partner 1

_____

Partner 2

*No such studies to this effect exist, to the best of our knowledge, which is very limited.

11.5 The Annoying Pet Peeves Contract

Use this life-altering contract to curb irksome things your partner does, such as talking too much, not talking enough (rare), loud food-chewing, jaw-clicking, and other unacceptable, hair-raising mouth sounds (too many to list here; there are so many . . . God, so many), nervous leg-bouncing, nervous pen-tapping, Jimmy legs (named after the great Jimmy Smits and referenced in *Seinfeld*), gross nail-biting, knuckle-cracking, back-cracking, overly indulgent "almost" masturbatory vibing-out-to-the-sound-of-the-white-noise-machine, etc.

_____ (Partner 1) and _____ (Partner 2), hereinafter referred to as "the Couple," hereby agree they will make a stupendous, relationship-saving effort to shut down behaviors that drive their partner insane and cause a series of quivering chills to shoot up their spine to their brainstem, nearly causing stroke. The behaviors to discontinue include _____, _____, _____, _____, _____, _____, and _____.

The Couple acknowledges that these behaviors are not only gross, they are also selfish and a direct insult to your Partner, especially after you have been notified that the actions/sounds/sights disgust your Partner. Each Partner agrees they can change and improve, and they accept this as an opportunity to become a better, more complete human being! The Couple will not resort to pathetic excuses for bull-shit behaviors, i.e., "I've been chewing loudly, clicking my jaw, and bouncing my legs like an asshole for years and years, most certainly since we met." Just because you're old doesn't mean you can't stop being a revolting freak. "But my jaw clicks and my throat grunts by itself; I have no control over it," you say stupidly, picking your nose. If

Stephen Hawking has managed to communicate using a single cheek muscle attached to a speech-generating machine, constituents of the Couple can find a way to stop making ultra-annoying noises through their orifices. If you can't, the relationship will either end or have an underlying tone of bitterness, resentment, and hatred. If you can stop shaking your legs and clicking your jaw, you will bask in bliss for eternity.

The undersigned faithfully enter into this contract on the ____ day of the month of _____, in the year _____. This contract never expires, dudes. If new behaviors are identified or appear in the place of successfully curbed behaviors, they can and should be eliminated as well for the health of the relationship and collective sanity.

I HAVE READ THIS AGREEMENT; I HAVE TAKEN TIME TO CONSIDER ITS IMPLICATIONS; I KNOW I DO ANNOYING, COMPULSIVE CRAP, BUT I CAN OVERCOME IT THROUGH SHEER FORCE OF WILL; I AGREE TO ITS TERMS; AND I VOLUNTARILY SUBMIT TO ITS EXECUTION.

_____

Partner 1

_____

Partner 2

11.6 The Welcome to the Doghouse Contract

So you didn't get to fix every problem area in your relationship with these contracts (we're genuinely shocked we didn't fix you), and you've had yourselves a fight. Maybe even an epic blowout that left one or both of you sucking both thumbs and weeping or singing the blues. Sorry! We really mean that. That said, let's define rules for how to punish each other for failing, including a limit on how long your partner can go on with their silent treatment.

_____ (Partner 1) and _____ (Partner 2), hereinafter referred to as "the Couple" agrees to take appropriate action to punish their partner when they are clearly the cause of a breakdown in the underpinnings of the relationship. These failures include breaking any contracts from this timeless book that the couple has signed, especially ones of vital importance such as _____, _____, _____, _____, and _____. Hey, Partners, we all make mistakes, so it's no big deal. That said, you receive an F on the aforementioned task(s), and you must now pay the piper. And he doesn't come cheap. He performs at high-profile reality star birthday parties, hardcore bat mitzvahs, White House events, white-noise parties/orgies, and every year, like clockwork, the AVN adult movie awards.

Now the "winning" partner is in a position of absolute power, and the "losing" partner must be taught a lesson. The loser will never learn if the punishment is not severe enough to "leave a mark"—on the psyche, of course. Punishments for failure to perform the requisite duties to maintain a healthy, happy relationship (again, including breaking one of the contracts of this book, which we take especially personally) shall consist of any one or combination of the following: _____, _____, _____, _____, _____, _____, and/or _____.

Additionally, controls must be put on the punishment so that your entire relationship does not become one extended S&M dungeon/dominatrix session. Or maybe that doesn't sound so bad to you. Whatever. The "winning partner" must refrain from _____, _____, and _____ during the punishment period (i.e., extended silent treatment, taunting, bringing mothers into it, actually feeding the contract breaker dog food that isn't human-grade, etc.). This breathtakingly wise contract shall expire after _____ days/hours/weeks (circle one).

I HAVE READ THIS AGREEMENT, I HAVE TAKEN TIME TO CONSIDER ITS IMPLICATIONS, I AGREE TO ACCEPT MY PUNISHMENT (LOSER) AND METE OUT PUNISHMENT WITHIN THE AFOREMENTIONED BOUNDS (WINNER), I AGREE TO ITS TERMS, AND I VOLUNTARILY SUBMIT TO ITS EXECUTION.

_____
Partner 1

_____
Partner 2

PART 12:
Pets, Friends, Kids, and Exes

These contracts are devoted to a mishmash of topics including pet hysteria, exes, friends, and having babies or not having babies. We hoped to touch on as many topics as possible, but really there's no end to crap to disagree on. By being more mindful of the stuff that bothers the hell out of your partner, and actually talking about and sorting out real-life stuff, your relationship can exist on a deeper level. Or if you break up, you can dunk this whole book in lighter fluid, tie it to a kettle bell, set it ablaze, and throw it through your now-ex's windshield. Either way, we hope it's proven helpful.

☐ 12.1 THE SHUT UP, MY CAT IS TRYING TO COMMUNICATE
WITH ME THROUGH HIS EYES CONTRACT

☐ 12.2 THE NO EXES CONTRACT

☐ 12.3 THE YOUR FRIENDS ARE TOTALLY THE BEST!
CONTRACT

☐ 12.4 THE WOULD BREEDING NOW BE APPROPRIATE?
CONTRACT

☐ 12.5 THE MAYBE WE SHOULDN'T BRING ANOTHER
PERSON INTO THIS WORLD CONTRACT

☐ 12.6 THE OUR KIDS ARE INSANE . . . LIKE CLINICALLY
DERANGED . . . I'M OUTTA HERE! CATCH YOU
ON THE FLIP SIDE CONTRACT

☐ 12.7 THE OUR CHILD'S FUTURE CONTRACT

12.1 The Shut Up, My Cat Is Trying to Communicate with Me through His Eyes Contract

Agree to make it seem less obvious that you like your #CatBoyfriend more than your partner. You can do it. Good human!

_____ (Partner 1) and _____ (Partner 2), hereinafter referred to as "the Couple," agree they will try to make it seem less obvious that they like their pet(s) more than they like one another on _____, the ____ day of the month of _____, in the year _____.

This contract bars Partners from consistently greeting their pet(s) with greater enthusiasm, creating social media posts that only ever feature their pet(s) and the great many dimensions to their unique bond as pet and owner, being so obsessed with an animal's "rescue" label to the point where nothing else in life is as important as their pet's earlier-in-life tribulations and their role as a savior (but of course, "Who saved whom?" as they say), _____, and _____.

If one Partner becomes clearly jealous of their loved one's deep bond with their pet(s), the offending Partner should take actions to stop neglecting their human lover. You may have heard comments like, "Jesus, you love that cat more than you love me" and, "Why don't you just marry the dog?" These may sound like straightforward, sensible observations and suggestions to the offending Partner, but they are actually sarcastic complaints that signify a problem.

The Couple will make their best efforts to spoil each other with attention, affection, and treats as much as they spoil their pets and will not put so much collective focus and energy into their pet(s) that the Relationship revolves around it/them and would easily become a quick dissolving goose egg sandwich in the absence of your fur baby(ies). Even though we all know that our furry friends are better and easier to relate to than people.

I HAVE READ THIS AGREEMENT, I HAVE TAKEN TIME TO CONSIDER ITS IMPLICATIONS, I FULLY UNDERSTAND ITS CONTENTS, I AGREE TO ITS TERMS, OUR CATS LOOK PISSED ABOUT THIS, AND I VOL-UNTARILY SUBMIT TO ITS EXECUTION.

_____
Partner 1

_____
Partner 2

12.2 The No Exes Contract

Do not discuss exes with your partner, ever. There is no reason to. Even if you are trashing them, it's still better not to go there. You've been warned. Use this contract and save a life.

_____ (Partner 1) and _____ (Partner 2), hereinafter referred to as "the Couple," declare they will never ever ever talk about their exes on _____, the ____ day of the month of _____, in the year ____. Partners are prohibited from talking about their exes, even a tiny, insignificant mention, as well as barred from telling stories that even marginally include their exes, even if it's hands-down the most funny, epic, apropos anecdote of all time. No.

Sure, you talked about it at first because one or both of you probably had just gotten out of a blah blah blah. Everyone has been hurt in a relationship. Everyone. You aren't special! Grow up! Thanks to the goddamn Internet, it's oh-so-easy to stalk your significant other's ex. Why would you want to do that? I don't know, to see how successful or skinny they are? Or to monitor their interactions, explore their corny hobbies, and critique their eyebrows, and we are not giving you blanks to fill out here, no sir. Could there be a bigger, sadder, more horrific time suck? We don't think so. The Couple agrees not to mention their exes or stalk each other's exes (or their own) because no good can come from any of this mess, and you know it. Now hurry, enough of this topic, move on to something else before you're hit with a huge, dark wave of insecurity and irrational jealousy! Go, go, go, go, go! Be gone!

I HAVE READ THIS AGREEMENT, I HAVE TAKEN TIME TO CONSIDER ITS IMPLICATIONS, I FULLY UNDERSTAND ITS CONTENTS, I AGREE

TO ITS TERMS, MY EX IS AN IRRELEVANT PIECE O' GARBAGE, FOR THE RECORD, AND I VOLUNTARILY SUBMIT TO ITS EXECUTION.

_____
Partner 1

_____
Partner 2

12.3 The Your Friends Are Totally the Best! Contract

Agree to behave as though you like your partner's friends even if they are the trashiest people you've ever met. Also, they probably don't like your pretentious, unfunny ass either! Let's all hang soon, XOXO!

_____ (Partner 1) and _____ (Partner 2), hereinafter referred to as "the Couple," declare they will go to great lengths to appear to like each other's friends on _____, the ____ day of the month of _____, in the year _____. This contract bars Partners from complaining about each other's friends, avoiding each other's friends, pretending to have business trips to Cleveland that are mysteriously canceled right around their partner's friend's birthday thing, acting like weird salty freaks around them (more than usual), shoving their hands into their own hair and shouting things like "This is torture!" _____, _____, and _____.

Partners will politely and respectfully point out why they might prefer not to hang out with each other's friends, at least not on a regular basis; and instead of being rude, Partners will take time to explain how they urgently must wash their hair that day or "study" or _____ instead of, for example, going to so-and-so's godforsaken Oscar party or World Cup viewing at some horribly loud pub that doesn't even have good food. What the hell?

The Couple acknowledges that because their respective friend groups seem to exist almost entirely of trashy douche bags or douchey snobs, they themselves probably aren't 100 percent completely unlike their friends. So try to find some common ground with these folks, because deep down, we are all douche bags. Wow, isn't that beautiful?

I HAVE READ THIS AGREEMENT, I HAVE TAKEN TIME TO CONSIDER ITS IMPLICATIONS, I FULLY UNDERSTAND ITS CONTENTS, I AGREE TO ITS TERMS, FINE, I WILL BE NICE TO MY PARTNER'S BUDS, AND I VOLUNTARILY SUBMIT TO ITS EXECUTION.

_____

Partner 1

_____

Partner 2

12.4 The Would Breeding Now Be Appropriate? Contract

Agree to have kids at some point. Huh? Because that's what people do. Right? Most people? I mean . . . doesn't your sister have kids? She likes them, right? She's happy with her life? Oh, your sister is in a behavioral health facility for suicidal ideation? Well, I'm sure things will be fine . . . let's impregnate each other! Sperm, I'd like you to meet egg!

_____ (Partner 1) and _____ (Partner 2), hereinafter referred to as "the Couple," declare they will seriously begin to try to have a kid by _____ (date/year) in the hopes that the world will become a more accepting, beautiful, enriching place and that we will all eventually be holding hands as we float off to heaven. Or at least that the average salary will be more than 1/1,000th of the average CEO salary. Having kids is the most wonderful thing you can do, you know? Forget about big oil and the Koch brothers and George Soros and global weirding. Again, it's the greatest thing you can do (we feel like if we keep repeating that we might start to believe it).

Disclaimer: It won't be the greatest thing if your kid turns out to be a moron and/or a brat. Nevertheless, the Couple agrees to go for it anyway. We, the Couple, enter into this contract on the ____ day of the month of _____, in the year _____. This contract is a serious one, so stipulations such as _____, _____, _____, and _____ can be added here to ensure this whole thing doesn't blow up in our face.

I HAVE READ THIS AGREEMENT, I HAVE TAKEN TIME TO CONSIDER ITS IMPLICATIONS, I FULLY UNDERSTAND ITS CONTENTS, I AGREE TO ITS TERMS, WE PRAY TO GOD COLLEGE WILL BECOME A RE-QUIRED GOVERNMENT-SUBSIDIZED, FREE ONLINE THING AND

WE WON'T HAVE TO GO INTO MASSIVE DEBT SO OUR CHILD CAN DECONSTRUCT THEIR SEXUALITY, AND I VOLUNTARILY SUBMIT TO ITS EXECUTION.

_____
Partner 1

_____
Partner 2

12.5 The Maybe We Shouldn't Bring Another Person into This World Contract

Agree never to have kids. We're making the world a better place one contract at a time; I think we can all agree on that.

_____ (Partner 1) and _____ (Partner 2), hereinafter referred to as "the Couple," declare they will not have kids, at least from _____ (date/year) to _____ (date/year), or never. Again, we acknowledge most kids really suck, especially in this day and age of Twitter, "snaps," uberPOOL, Facebook (ha, just kidding, no one uses Facebook anymore but the joke is on us and Zuckerberg's neighbors, whether that be in Hawaii, Spain, Ireland, South Africa, Bermuda, Dakar, Abu Dhabi, Russia, San Francisco, or hell).

But seriously (and this book is serious, if nothing else), if these are the people we now look to for insight and guidance on where our "culture" is headed, we should probably all join celibate hermit cults or at least agree that our beautiful loins need to be kept in check for a while, at least until "we figure out what is going on." Let's be cautious about this whole breeding thing that everyone makes such a fuss about. We make this holding off on / never having children vow on _____, the ____ day of the month of _____, in the year _____. The Contract (also known as The Gird & Guard Your Loins Contract) bars the Couple from impregnating one another until the time is right—which, again, could very well be never, and the Couple is cool with that.

I HAVE READ THIS AGREEMENT, I HAVE TAKEN TIME TO CONSIDER ITS IMPLICATIONS, I FULLY UNDERSTAND ITS CONTENTS, I AGREE

TO ITS TERMS, I WOULD MAKE A HORRENDOUS PARENT, AND I
VOLUNTARILY SUBMIT TO ITS EXECUTION.

_____

Partner 1

_____

Partner 2

12.6 The Our Kids Are Insane . . . Like Clinically Deranged . . . I'm Outta Here! Catch You on the Flip Side Contract

Kids are great. So amazing, right? Some are even objectively cute, although we've found that to be rare. Maybe four in thirty-seven? Anyhow, by the age of two or three, kids can get really annoying. Filled with wonderment and enchantment? Sure. Annoying as all holy hell? You bet. So this contract will set the terms of each parent getting a free pass / escape / get out of jail free card from the hell that can be child rearing.

_____ (Partner 1) and _____ (Partner 2), hereinafter referred to as "the Couple," hereby declare to grant each other one free pass, i.e., a break of the duration of _____ (hours/days) to escape our sporadically horrific child(ren), whom we of course love very much (it feels right to add that, or else we'd sound like bad people) every _____ days/weeks (circle one). This free time, during which you can "get in touch" with who you were before this/these maniac(s) came barreling into your life, can be spent in the house, out of the house, in the car crying, in a Chipotle crying, in a Dunkin' Donuts laughing, in a Target spending frantically and/or crying, in a Starbucks eating a Protein Bistro Box dazed, in a bar drinking, laughing, and curled up in the fetal position, _____, _____, _____, or _____. Options are basically unlimited, although the free-pass partner may not see a prostitute (right?), flee to Canada (Mexico would be OK in some cases, depending on what you bring back), _____, _____, or _____. This contract goes into effect on _____, the ____ day of the month of _____, in the year of _____.

This contract will expire on _____ ("never" is surely an option, or until the kids move out, which may also be never / upon your death—they'll still live in your house, but you will mercifully have passed on to the next realm).

I HAVE READ THIS AGREEMENT, I HAVE TAKEN TIME TO CONSIDER ITS IMPLICATIONS, I AM STILL A GOOD MOTHER/FATHER, OR AT LEAST I WILL CONTINUE TO TELL MYSELF THAT (HEY, IN THE OL' DAYS PEOPLE BARELY EVEN ACKNOWLEDGED THEIR KIDS' EXISTENCE, AND THAT WAS OK, WASN'T IT?), I FULLY UNDERSTAND ITS CONTENTS, I AGREE TO ITS TERMS, AND I VOLUNTARILY SUBMIT TO ITS EXECUTION.

_____
Partner 1

_____
Partner 2

12.7 The Our Child's Future Contract

The cost of college has flown off the handle, gone beyond absurd. It is the devil's work. College "endowments" and student debt continue to rise, college grads are becoming douchier and more useless and self-absorbed by the semester. So you, as caring parents, could start saving right now and still fall woefully short of paying your child's tuition and end up in a "van down by the river." (Sounds nice, actually; like a decent-shape RV? Nice.) Or you could try to direct your child(ren) down another career path, such as untrained circus clown (the circus is closing, but they could still do it without the elephants, right?).

_____ (Partner 1) and _____ (Partner 2), hereinafter referred to as "the Couple," hereby vow to take measures to save _____ dollars / euros / pesos / dinar / shekels / florin / francs / nafkas / birr / tenges / shillings / kroner / _____ (we're expecting this book to go global . . . so just circle one) in order to provide for the educational future of our spawn. Lord knows what that future holds. Look at this last election and the Cubs' World Series win. It's chaos. The Couple agrees to save some cash in the off chance that the apocalypse is _not_ upon us. We, the Couple, also vow to encourage our child to follow our innate interests, such as _____, _____, _____, and _____ or push them toward something more in line with what we want and what will help them maybe even pay for their own education/training, such as _____, _____, or _____. This contract, hereafter referred to as the "They're Our Kids, Yes, But That Doesn't Mean We Have to Sacrifice Our Retirement for Them Contract" or the "Let's Have Our Kids Actually Contribute to Society in a Meaningful Way, and Not by Coding for Ten Hours a Day at Some Idiotic, Reprobate Social

Media Company" goes into effect on _____, the ____ day of the month of _____, in the year of _____.

I HAVE READ THIS AGREEMENT, I HAVE TAKEN TIME TO CONSIDER ITS IMPLICATIONS, MY KIDS ARE INDIVIDUALS BUT THAT DOES NOT MEAN WE CAN'T STEER THEM TOWARD A CAREER THAT WILL ENHANCE OUR OWN FINANCIAL SITUATION, I FULLY UNDERSTAND ITS CONTENTS, I AGREE TO ITS TERMS, AND I VOLUNTARILY SUBMIT TO ITS EXECUTION.

_____

Partner 1

_____

Partner 2